300 Weekend Decorating Ideas

Contents

100 Weekend Decorating Ideas

100 Big Style, Small Rooms Ideas

100 Weekend Wall Ideas

Weekend
Decorating

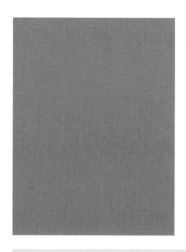

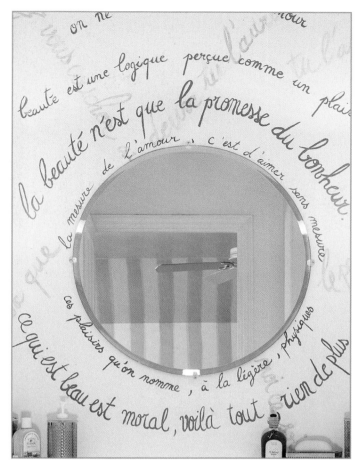

Decorating doesn't have to be time-consuming

or expensive. You can breathe new life into your home's interiors by choosing a few simple projects that will have a big impact on the way a room looks and feels. Window and wall treatments, floor coverings, furniture, and decorative accessories all help shape mood and style; altering any one can energize a setting.

If the neutrals you once found serene now seem a bit boring, check out "Coloring Class" beginning on *page 8*. Rich, vibrant hues adorn the walls in every room of the modest California cottage spotlighted in the chapter.

Are you interested in reenergizing your walls with the latest glazing or stenciling techniques? See the "Wonderful Walls" featured on *pages 74–77*. If your interiors are in need of architectural embellishment, consider adding a few of the decorative molding treatments shown on *pages 44–4;* then give your mantel a makeover as shown on *pages 48–49*.

Do you have some comfy furnishings in need of coverings? See "Simple Slipcovers" beginning on *page 40*. Maybe a new furniture arrangement is all you really need. You'll find ideas in the before-and-after room schemes featured on *pages 24–29*.

And there is much more—100 ideas in all for decorating and updating your home are included in this section alone, and almost every project can be completed in a weekend or less. So turn the page, get your creative juices flowing, and grab your gear. There's some simply sensational weekend decorating to be done!

Pillow Power

ADD COLOR AND TEXTURE TO YOUR DECOR WITH A STACK OF THROW PILLOWS. A single pillow—or perhaps a matching pair—adds a subtle touch of color to a sofa or love seat; for more color, step up to three to five pillows. Mix and match florals, plaids, checks, and solids. To ensure the fabrics complement one another, choose patterns of different sizes and use color as a unifying factor. Give purchased pillows a personalized look with buttons, bows, ribbons, or fringe. For extra panache, sprinkle a few new accessories, such as vases, floral arrangements, and throws, into the room in colors that coordinate with the new pillows. These simple changes provide quick, affordable ways to match your decor to any season.

1 A REAL SHAM
For a quick makeover, slip pillows into tailored, button-down shams. They're easy to make at a fraction of the cost of ready-made shams, and you can match them to bedding or upholstery. Pillow and sham patterns and pillow forms are available at fabrics stores.

2
SUITE COLOR

In this sunny master retreat, throw pillows trimmed with yellow fringe accentuate the wall color. Additional pillows introduce an accent of green. A second set of similar pillows softens the window seat. A dabbling of new green accessories carries the green throughout the suite.

3
BURLAP BEAUTY

An unexpected combination of natural burlap and bronze-color silk edging adorns the window-seat cushion in this living room. A print fabric in earthy tones dresses up the center of the coordinating burlap pillow. Buttons and bows finish off the edges of the sewn-on design.

Coloring Class

YOUR HOUSE CAN GO FROM BASIC TO BEAUTIFUL IN ONE OR TWO WEEKENDS. CHOOSE YOUR OVERALL COLOR SCHEME from a favorite painting, fabric, floral arrangement, or collectible. If the colors work well together in the piece, they will also work well

together in your home. In this California cottage, the palette for the entire home was pulled from the fabric used in the living room window treatment: sunshine yellow, watermelon red, and periwinkle blue. To ensure a match with the fabric, the owner took a swatch to the paint store and had custom colors made. This service is typically free.

4
SHADE SECRETS

Before you put brush to wall, purchase small amounts of paint to apply to poster boards. Place the painted boards in the rooms you plan to paint. Review the colors throughout the day to ensure you've chosen the proper shades. Note that when the paint covers all the walls in a room, it often appears a shade or two darker.

TWO TONES Separate bright hues with a stripe of white to create the illusion of a border and molding treatment. To ensure your choices look good together, select hues within the same color family, such as brights or pastels.

5

ART WORKS
Complementary artwork and accessories make wall colors pop. In this part of the living room, a collection of dog prints keeps the atmosphere bright and the spirit light. Flowers and glassware also display dazzling primary colors. While some matching is good, don't make every accessory exactly the same color. Items a shade or two lighter or darker add welcome variety.

7
WHITE PLUS ONE

If the thought of filling your home with primary hues seems overwhelming, consider this coloring scheme. White when combined with one other color is fail-safe and easy to accessorize. If you want to keep things light, use white or a white-background print on the walls. For a bolder look, choose a darker solid-color background and white furnishings. In this cottage kitchen, blue walls and white cabinets are accented with touches of yellow.

8

KEEP IT GOING
In small homes with open plans, choose a whole-house coloring scheme that flows seamlessly from room to room. In this house of a little more than 900 square feet, the blue used on the kitchen walls is repeated on the walls of the master bedroom; here, however, yellow, instead of white, serves as the primary accent color.

Window Dressing

NOTHING ADDS MORE DESIGN FLAIR TO A ROOM THAN THE RIGHT WINDOW TREATMENT. CHOOSE TREATMENTS TO HIGHLIGHT OR ENHANCE YOUR HOME'S architectural style, warm or cool a room, and even camouflage an imperfection or two. The featured treatments offer extraordinary style in a range of designs to fit almost any motif. Choose from rope-edged silk panels, linen Roman shades, custom-decorated roller shades, painted glass panes, or open shelves installed inside a box-shaped bay. To narrow selections to the perfect one for each setting, choose a look that also meets your needs for privacy, light, and air flow.

STYLISH SILK

Sew simple hemmed panels from silk fabric. Depending on window locations, cut the panels so they are approximately 6 inches longer and at least twice the width of the window you are covering. Press under all edges ½ inch, then turn under the sides and bottom again an additional 2½ inches. Turn under the top 1½ inches more; then press and sew all hems. Whipstitch braided rope across the top of the panel, creating loops for hanging at equal intervals. Slip loops over a bamboo rod.

9

10 ROMAN FERNS

Install Roman shades inside window casings to show off woodwork. This shade *opposite* is made from white linen adorned with a fern motif. Stenciling a plain fabric roller shade creates a similar effect. For added softness, arrange the shade's bottom edge into a soft curve, then sew the edge in place.

SHADY CHARACTERS

Dress up a plain roller shade with printouts of your favorite people. Photocopy images onto plain white paper, then trim to size. Color the borders of the copied photos with markers and use a spray adhesive to attach the copies to the shade. Brush on a matte medium to protect the photos.

12

WALL SCARVES 11

Adorn both walls and windows with sheer panels tacked at the ceiling line. The 26-inch-wide panels are 5 inches longer than the walls so that they puddle onto the floor.

13 TEXTURAL TEAM

Mix the pattern and texture of fabrics in your color palette to create visual variety. In the bedroom *opposite*, the panels are made from rustic burlap trimmed with elegant paisley velvet. The tab-top valance above the desk is made from the same velvet fabric.

PRIVACY GLASS

Stencil a pattern onto glass panes to create privacy without blocking the light. Clean the window with ammonia, then stencil with paint formulated for humid areas.

15

14

MAP MAJOR

Hang an antique map as a window shade. Both ends of this map are wrapped around wooden dowels; the top dowel is mounted inside the window frame with metal brackets.

16 SUN SHELVES

Use wood screws to attach wire mesh shelves to the interior of window casings, then fill the shelves with favorite collectibles. These shelves show off birdhouses. Colorful glass vases would look equally attractive sparkling in the sunlight.

Easy

PUT TOGETHER ONE OF THESE EASY-TO-MAKE OTTOMANS IN JUST A FEW HOURS. THEN SPEND YOUR SPARE TIME SEEING HOW WELL IT HOLDS UP YOUR FEET. Give your three-season porch a touch of color, or grace a plain living room with a dabble of sunshine yellow. Make matching ottomans to place in front of the fireplace for an extra seating area, or cover a broken-in footrest with a sheer slipcover. The colorful ottomans featured here are ideal for holding a glass of lemonade, a board game, or a pair of tired feet. Each ottoman begins with materials as ordinary as plywood, foam, fabric, and prefinished legs. For easy-to-follow instructions on how to make these ottomans, see pages 91–92.

17
PRETTY PASTELS

The mismatched ottomans *opposite* pack a fun summertime punch. The fabrics shown are new cotton blends. Vintage tablecloths also work well as ottoman covers. For best results, choose sturdy washable fabrics.

Ottomans

NO-FUSS CUBES
19

Felt squares and layers of foam make these fun block-shape ottomans fast to finish. They're perfect for holding up board games or as secondary seating options in front of a fireplace or other cozy spot. Punch them up with primary colors or tone them down with an earthy palette.

SIMPLE SLIPS
18

If your present ottoman works great but looks tacky, give it new life with a simple-to-sew slipcover. For added summer color, accent the walls with an easy-sew sheer curtain to match the ottoman. As summer turns to autumn, you can replace the curtain and slipcover with more seasonal fabrics and colors, then add throws and cushions to fit the scheme.

Making Arrangements

IF YOUR DINING ROOM AND FAMILY ROOM LOOK LIKE EVERYONE ELSE'S IN THE NEIGHBORHOOD, RESTYLE THEM INTO INVITING RETREATS by arranging your existing furniture, art, and accessories in more pleasing ways. Start by looking to the architecture of a room to find a focal point. In a room that lacks a natural focus, as often is the case in a rectangular dining room, create a center of attention with furnishings or artwork, then arrange everything else around the new focal point. When arranging the living or family room, avoid pushing furniture against the wall; instead, center or angle sofas and chairs in front of the fireplace or media center. To update art and accessories, look in adjoining rooms and storage areas. By moving items from one spot to another, you can create a fresh look without spending a penny.

Before

DASHING DINING
Before its decorative redo, the dining room at *left* lacked pizzazz—rectangles and shiny surfaces dominated the space. In the rearranged room *opposite,* the dining table becomes the focal point simply by being angled below the existing chandelier. Adding burlap shades and a jute rug and replacing a mirror with a colorful piece of art from an adjacent room give the space more color and texture. A billowing table runner and a contemporary centerpiece encompassing spheres and stars further soften the room's rectilinear lines.

Before

FIREPLACE FOCAL POINT

Moving a mirror from the dining
room wall to above the living
room fireplace makes the mantel
top seem larger and increases its
visual importance. A second
piece of framed art stacked
against the mirror adds depth
and color, as does a colorful vase
filled with a few simple flowers.
Angling the upholstered pieces
around the mantel further
emphasizes the fireplace and
keeps the overall arrangement
from looking too rectangular.

22

DEN DO-OVER

When building your own room arrangements, create visual interest throughout the room with art, accessories, and botanicals positioned in the shape of a triangle. In the den at *left*, artwork, plants, and accessories create decorative peaks and valleys. As in the other rooms, furnishings are angled to the walls, instantly creating more shape and visual interest. This arrangement also provides a clear view of the media center (not shown) from every seat.

Before

23 STAIR STEPS

A plain wall adjacent to a staircase can become a gallery for favorite photos. The photos ascend at the same degree as the stairs and draw attention to the stairwell. Oversized mats and identical white frames give the photographs prominence.

Picture This

ARRANGING ARTWORK CAN BE ONE OF THE MOST DAUNTING DECORATING TASKS. These examples illustrate stylish solutions. A rule of thumb is to place artwork at eye level, but don't let that guideline limit your imagination. Hanging artwork a bit lower can create a more intimate feel. Before you get out the hammer and nails, arrange your pieces on a large sheet of paper on the floor until you have a visually appealing grouping. Trace the outline of the frames onto the paper, then use the paper as a map for nail holes: Tape the marked paper onto the wall, nail through the outlined frames, and then remove the paper.

SHELVE IT 24
Increase your display space by installing a long narrow shelf, then layer on art and collectibles in easily changeable, eye-pleasing ways. Hang other favorites on the wall itself; emphasize a small photo by encompassing it in another frame.

REFINE IT 25
Arrange different-size frames as you would a jigsaw puzzle. For a crisp, more refined look, choose all-white frames and mats. This bright connection helps tie the images together without overpowering the individual photographs.

26 REPEAT IT

Arrange similar works at equal distances from each other to create a stunning focal point. When deciding how many prints to hang, consider the room's scale and the complexity of the decor. Large groupings look best in simply adorned rooms.

MAKE IT ODD

Work in odd numbers, such as sets of threes, fives, and sevens. In the vignette *below*, seven elements—one main print in the center and three elements on each side—create a complex yet visually pleasing display.

27

PLAY FAVORITES

Install picture ledges to make small framed pictures and collectibles stand out. When working on a ledge display, pick a theme and let it guide you. The display *above* features shades of gray.

28

ACCENT WINDOWS

Use artwork to connect and complement window treatments. Here, two identically framed teacup prints pair with a side chair to create an attractive grouping.

29

30
THINK BIG

To gain the most visual impact from your mantel, top it with artwork or mirrors that match the massiveness of the space. In this living room, the oversize artwork draws the eye up to the high ceiling.

Dynamic Dining

RECAST A BASIC DINING ROOM INTO A WELCOMING GATHERING SPACE WITH AFFORDABLE FIX-UPS. If a new dining set isn't in the budget, restyle the table and chairs you already have (or a flea-market find) into something that better suits your tastes with slipcovers and a full-length tablecloth. Add drama with a new light fixture or an étagère to show off collectibles or dinnerware. Create architectural interest by installing wainscoting and crown molding—do-it-yourself kits are available at home centers. Complete your makeover with the perfect table setting, including fresh flowers and attractive linens. For more information on slipcovering chairs, see pages 40–43 and 92–93.

NEUTRAL ZONE

Soft taupes and creams cover these dining room walls, window valances, curtain panels, and even the table and chairs *opposite*. A wainscoting kit adds architectural interest, and crown molding gives a sense of height to standard 8-foot ceilings. An arched-top window frame, purchased from a salvage yard and stained mocha brown, serves as wall art.

31

GETTING
WARMER Verdant-
colored walls make the white
woodwork and built-in corner
cabinet in this dining room pop.
Painting the interior of the
built-in red raises the piece to
focal-point status. Upholstered
cornices make the windows
appear taller, and slipcovers give
the captain's chairs even greater
importance. A width of burlap
trimmed with a stripe of red linen
teams with a geometric print to
make a colorful,
inexpensive
table runner.

32

TABLE TOPPERS

If time or budget constraints limit your dining room decorating possibilities, set your sights on the tabletop. You can update the look of the room in minutes with a new tablecloth, fresh flowers, and pretty plates. To make your decorating decisions easier, first choose the blooms. They can help dictate your color scheme and accessories, and even affect your menu selections.

In the dining room *opposite*, delicate violets serve as the decorative starting point. **(33)** Adorn a bakery cheesecake with a crown of edible flowers and serve it on a glass plate stacked atop a favorite pottery vase. **(34)** Send messages of friendship with tussie-mussies: Tie one of these small handheld arrangements to the back of each guest's chair. **(35)** Press flowers between a clear dessert plate and a pastel dinner plate to make each place setting one-of-a-kind. **(36)** Corral silverware in paper that has been folded and decorated to resemble seed packets.

Simple Slipcovers

WHETHER YOU WANT TO RESCUE DINGY OR DATED CHAIRS OR CHANGE THE LOOK OF YOUR ROOM TO MATCH THE SEASON,

there's a slipcover for the job. Replace heavily patterned winter fabrics with refreshing white and pastel prints for spring. Meld old furnishings with new, cover tattered seat cushions, or transform a folding chair into a seat attractive enough for a wedding reception. Also, kids and slipcovers make a smart match—when the former gets the latter dirty, soap and water provide a quick cleanup. For advice on how to make slipcovers, see pages 92–93.

NAPKIN COVER-UP

Dress an everyday dining chair for a special occasion with a seat cover made from two printed napkins. For added glitz, edge the napkins with gold trim, decorative braiding, and tassels. Use remaining napkins to adorn the tabletop and line bread baskets.

37

38 FLIRTY SKIRT

No chair is too old for this little number. Show off shapely legs and a pretty back by fashioning a short skirt into a standard box-pleat design. To ensure the skirt and bows keep their shape, slip lightweight florist's wires between the fabric layers.

39 CHAIR CAPS

These sheer caps *below* slip over chair backs for an elegant flourish. You can modify the design for other chair styles. For an extraspecial occasion, make caps to match the wall scarves featured on page 17, and then arrange furnishings as suggested on page 25 to give your dining room a fresh new look.

40 CHAIR DRAPE

For a fresh summer look, cut two draping chair covers and a table runner from a purchased tablecloth. No sewing is required—you can use either glue or hem tape to finish the edges. As decorative touches, adorn your new tablecloth creations with buttons, rickrack, and leaves stamped from fabric paint.

41 CLASSIC COVER-UP

Give your dining room an elegant, tailored look with classic full-length chair covers. Covers are available for purchase in many home decorating catalogs, or you can make your own following the directions on pages 92–93.

Architectural Accents

ADD CHARACTER AND CHARM TO ANY ROOM IN YOUR HOME WITH THE LOOK OF MOLDING.

Paint, wall coverings, and stock moldings can create versions of chair rails, crown moldings, or wall-paneling treatments in just a few hours. To achieve a classic designer look, choose a decorative molding commonly found in homes built during the same era as yours. The most effective enhancements look as if they've always been part of the room's architecture.

42
WALL ART

A combination of red wallpaper rectangles gives the flat walls of the bedroom at *left* architectural interest. Create a similar effect by taping off the desired-size rectangles with painter's tape and then filling in the lines with the desired paint color. To achieve a raised paneling effect, you'll need to paint three rectangles per section.

3-D DINING
Picture-frame molding, purchased from a home center, accentuates similarly framed prints and gives this rectangular dining room needed dimension. The prefinished bamboolike molding was attached to the walls with finishing nails. A painted pattern on the wooden floor creates the impression of a fine Asian rug without the worry of upkeep. For additional floor makeover ideas, see "Fabulous Floors" on pages 62–65.

43

44

PAPER PLAY
A bamboolike textured paper covers the lower two-thirds of the walls in this dining room. Two sets of matching borders cover the top third, creating the illusion of multiple decorative moldings.

45

MOLDING MAKEOVER

Stock molding pieces, purchased unfinished from a home center, were cut, primed, and painted, then nailed to the wall above the mantel to create a focal point in the living room *left*. The new moldings blend well with the existing fireplace surround and molding treatments.

Mantel Makeovers

GIVE YOUR FIREPLACE MANTEL A FRESH NEW FACE WITH AN ARRANGEMENT THAT LOOKS nothing like the next-door neighbor's. Relegate the candlesticks to a tabletop and your artwork to a different room, then express yourself in a whole new way. Set off collections of greeting cards, miniatures, or photos with shadow boxes and artist's easels. If your hobby is gardening, top off the mantel with a trio of window boxes.

46

INSIDE THE BOX
Black and white display pieces—shadow boxes and picture frames—create a striking display for a camera and black-and-white photo collection. The mounted pieces fill the wall and support items both inside and outside the box. Postcards taped inside the decorative wood molding complete the look.

Before

Before

47

GARDEN GROWN
Shiny aluminum planters filled with real grass adorn this summer-fresh mantel top. Burlap runners hang over the mantel's edge and warm up the white. Glass cookie jars filled with silk flowers hang from wires and ribbons attached to screws in the crown molding.

Kitchen Capers

REVAMP YOUR KITCHEN WITHOUT BREAKING THE BUDGET BY USING HOME-CENTER BUYS AND SALVAGE FINDS IN UNEXPECTED WAYS. Enliven the overall look of the room by painting the inner part of raised panel doors a different color. Disguise less-than-perfect cupboards with framed art, such as botanical prints, family photos, or pages from an old calendar or book. Increase storage by installing painted shelves topped with stacks of wicker baskets, then stencil a salvaged desk and a home-center wall cabinet to match for a custom message center. Still have energy? Adorn your backsplash with a combination of broken and decorative tiles, then transform a basic kitchen cabinet into an attractive display by adding glass-inset doors.

49

COLORFUL CUBBIES
For extra decorating pizzazz, paint the interiors of open shelves one color and the front trim boards a contrasting one. Fill each open cubby with a tall rectangular basket, then use the baskets to store dry goods, veggies, or linens.

PERFECT PICTURES
To give flat-door cupboards, *opposite*, the look of raised panels, frame your favorite photos or prints in identical fashion, matching the frame sizes to the sizes of the center panels on the cabinet doors. Drill pilot holes into the sides of the frames and through the doors, then secure the frames to the doors with drywall screws. When you tire of the prints, you can replace them with new images.

48

HOT TOPICS

50

Warm up a too-cool kitchen by painting the walls citrus yellow and staining the cabinets with a vibrant red wash. If you are restaining your wood cabinets, you may need to strip off the old stain first. Test your new stain color on the inside of a door until you're satisfied with the color combination. Apply the new stain with a lint-free cloth, then let the finish dry thoroughly. Add design dash to the backsplash by installing a mosaic of broken tiles interspersed with decoratively painted whole tiles.

WIRE WONDERS

To make a small kitchen feel more open, cut out the center panels on upper cabinet doors and insert wire mesh, available in rolls at home centers. If you don't have the tools to make your own door cuts, take the doors to a cabinetmaker or replace a few doors with those designed for glass inserts.

51

52

PAINTED PANELS

Remove the cabinet doors you want to update, then sand, prime, and paint the inner parts of the panel doors. While the paint is still wet, use a second, dry paintbrush to create the strié effect *above;* let dry. Apply polyurethane to protect the finish; let dry again. Then rehang the doors.

53

COLOR CONNECTION

Give unrelated pieces the look of a matching set by painting a funky finish, then distressing it with sandpaper. Sea green paint, block-patterned stripes, and an artichoke stencil create a folk art look for a cupboard and desk set, *left.*

Alfresco Entertaining

INVITE GUESTS FOR A SPECIAL TREAT: A GET-TOGETHER IN THE GARDEN. Move a table and chairs from your porch to a scenic spot, then make the ambience special by using your favorite table service and an enchanting topiary as decoration. Hang

a pretty candelabra from a tree branch, or create instant shade with a hand-painted umbrella.

HIGH TEA

An ivy-entwined plate stand and fine china bring the elegance of an English garden to the backyard. The topiary shown at *left* and *far left* was created with a salvaged étagère. A three-tier plate rack can be substituted. Place a pot of ivy on the bottom tier and braid the plant strands up each side.

54

PRETTY PITCHER

Use specialty glass-painting markers or heat-set acrylics and stencils—all available at crafts stores—to customize a clear pitcher and glasses.

55

56

FLORAL TRAY

Prime, paint, and stencil an unfinished wooden tray, and let it dry. Then randomly glue flat-sided marbles between the flowers. Protect your work and create a flat serving surface by lining the interior of the tray with a piece of clear acrylic plastic.

57

SHADE MAKER

Adorn a natural canvas umbrella with hand-painted or stenciled flowers. To make painting easier, place the open umbrella in its stand using just one section of pole; that way, the canvas is low enough to be reached comfortably.

58 OUTDOOR CHANDELIER

Candlelight whispers romance. Shop for a candle chandelier, *left*, at stores that sell garden ornaments. Ask a hardware store to cut a chain to the length you'll need to attach the chandelier to a tree with S-hooks. Make sure that the candles fit securely into the individual holders and there is at least 5 feet of clearance between the tree branches and the flames.

59 ROSE CANDELABRA

To decorate an outdoor candelabra, cut roses and place them on florist's picks. Fill small terra-cotta pots with florist's foam. Push the picks into the foam, and cover with moss. Intersperse the pots of roses with pots of English ivy to twine through the candelabra. For a twist on tradition, use votive candles instead of tapers.

60 WINDOW POTS

Instead of a standard window box, adorn your windowsills with pretty pots. The containers at *left* are sap buckets attached to the sill with nails driven through holes that were originally intended to hold the buckets to maple trees.

61 BIKE PLANTER

For a few dollars, you can purchase a rusty old bike from a flea market. Attach a front basket and fill it with begonias, *above*. For added interest, intertwine vines into the wheel spokes.

62 TRELLIS SWING
Create a garden swing by topping sturdy store-bought trellises with a homemade canvas awning. A roof-shape wood frame, made from 2×4 and 4×4 boards, holds up the swing and keeps the awning in place. Lots of plump cushions and a nearby basket of goodies invite relaxation.

SOUTHERN GENTILITY

Table linens make outdoor dining even better. This tablecloth has been paint-stamped with daisies. For a charming touch, adorn the chair backs with inexpensive, wide-brimmed straw hats, and use acrylic paints to transform an ordinary clay pot into an attractive centerpiece. Complete the breezy look with a pitcher of lemonade and a cake decorated with frosting daisies.

Fabulous Floors

TURN OLD PLANKS INTO WORTHY WALKWAYS WITH THESE IMPRESSIVE WOOD-FLOOR FINISHES. Stencil on rectangles to create the look of a rug, add a motif to set off a reading nook, or create a checkerboard to hide imperfections. Before you stencil, wood floors should be sanded, stained, and sealed with one coat of polyurethane, then lightly sanded again to give the surface some "tooth." When stenciling patterns with multiple overlays, apply paint or stain to all of the first overlay area, then paint or stain all of the next overlay area. Once the layered design is finished, seal the floor with two coats of polyurethane.

64 DIAMOND WASH After a light sanding and thorough cleaning, alternating squares for this diamond-pattern floor *above* and *opposite* were taped off and left as is. The remaining squares were covered with a light coating of watered-down latex paint.

65 BARE TREADS
Stair treads once covered by old carpeting take on a new look with simple sanding, priming, and painting, *below left*. Freehand vines and doodads disguise nail holes and other imperfections. Polyurethane protects the pink stripes and white background.

TILE LOOK-ALIKE
From a distance, this painted floor *above right* resembles mosaic tiles. A putty-color base coat and sponge-painted squares form the intricate design, created in just a weekend. 66

BORDER BEAUTY

A stenciled border, *below right*, gives wooden flooring a decorative lift. Stencils were taped to the floor in even increments, then stencil-painting creme was applied using a stenciling brush to fill in the pattern. Top-coat spray protects the painted design.

68

67

UNDER COVER

Cleaning, priming, and painting plywood subflooring creates a rustic-looking background for the master bedroom floor *above left*. The overlay design was done freehand using an artist's brush and thinned latex paint. Slight wobbles in the final outcome add character and an appearance of age. Two coats of polyurethane protect the painted finish.

Great Divides

A SIMPLE FOLDING SCREEN CAN BLOCK LIGHT, PROTECT PRIVACY, OR SPICE UP A DULL CORNER. CREATE ONE OF YOUR OWN TO FIT the space you have available and to match your decor. The screen at *left* is made from decorative grilles sized for a French door. The wooden frames are connected with hinges and adorned with decorative papers hot-glued to the backs of the individual grilles. This folding screen and the two featured on the following pages were completed in no more than a day and for less than $100. Doors, grilles, and hinges are available at home centers.

ASIAN-INSPIRED

Ready-made door grilles combine with decorative papers from a crafts store to create the lightweight, transparent shoji screen at *left*. To make a similar screen, prime and spray-paint standard French door grilles, then cut papers to fit, adding ¼ inch to each measurement. Glue the right side of each paper to a grille, on the side that normally faces the glass.

69

70 DREAMY DOORS

The screen *opposite* is made from two sets of bifold doors, such as those used for closets. An additional set of hinges connects the door sets. To create the cloudlike finish, the doors were primed, painted blue, and then textured by scrunching cheesecloth into a slightly lighter-color paint diluted with water and dabbing it onto the panels. Stenciled-on leaves complete the look.

71 TOILE TALES

Pink toile fabric covers the folding screen *above*. Like the screen *opposite*, the four-panel screen was made by connecting two sets of bifold doors with additional hinges. The fabric was cut to fit each panel with a 1-inch seam allowance. Fabric edges were overlapped and folded under to create a neat edge and then stapled at the top, bottom, and both sides of each panel. Crisscross ribbons, also stapled at the panel's edges, hold photos and notes.

Wake-Up Calls

BORED WITH YOUR PLAIN BED? ENERGIZE YOUR BEDROOM DECOR AND INVIGORATE WAKE-UP TIME WITH ONE OF THESE SPICY ALTERNATIVES TO TRADITIONAL HEADBOARDS. Unusual yet reasonably priced materials such as chair cushions, coffee sacks, and fabric panels offer standout style and can be personalized to match any decor. If you can't find a fabric you like, purchase a set of matching twin-size sheets or a twin-size bedspread to use as coverings for your headboard panels. Each head-of-the-bed treatment shown can be made in only a few hours. No sewing is required.

PILLOW POWER

Soften your notion of headboards with this treatment *opposite* that transforms simple chair cushions into a decorative wall treatment. Loops sewn from the cushion's chair ties are hung from a decorative curtain rod attached to the wall a few feet above the head of the bed.

72

COFFEE KLATCH
Waken to the smell of coffee before you even start brewing it. This simple headboard is made from large burlap coffee–bean sacks attached to foam-covered plywood rectangles. These boards measure 15×18 inches and are covered with 2-inch-thick foam stapled to the back of each board. A second covering of colorful coffee sacks completes the rich and creamy look.

PRETTY PANELS

74

Embellish a once-blank wall with fabric-covered panels sized to complement your bed's dimensions and ceiling height. The panels *above* adorn a standard double bed and measure 2×4½ feet each. For added interest, the panels were made from two fabrics, then stapled to the back of the boards, which are hung from the walls with screws.

75 WALL ART

Accentuate framed prints by surrounding each with a second frame painted onto the wall. Create the look of wainscoting by coating the lower third of the wall with an accent color and adding a stenciled or stamped border just above it.

Wonderful Walls

WHIP UP WALLS THAT SHOUT ORIGINALITY WITH THESE SIMPLE, HANDS-ON PROJECTS.

Experiment with bold colors, or mix paint with glaze to create a soft, translucent effect. Try stenciling, stamping, or striping the hallway or bath walls; then use a squeegee to create a gingham check in the master suite.

Still not satisfied? Form an elegant diamond pattern on the living room walls or adorn the dining room with sophisticated scrolls. Highlight treasured prints in the breakfast room by surrounding each three-dimensional frame with a two-dimensional version, then add a hand-painted border. Each of our featured projects can be accomplished in just a day or two by even a novice painter, and you'll be able to impress your friends with the professional appearance of your results. For easy-to-follow directions on how to paint walls decoratively, see pages 94–95.

FLOWER FIELDS

Roll on a roomful of pretty petals in two easy steps: Stencil on a pastel shade, then follow with a darker accent. The even placement of the flowers results in a finished room that looks professionally wallpapered.

76

SCROLLS

Bring definition to plain walls with tone-on-tone vertical stripes and a hand-painted scroll border. The scrolls at *right* were drawn with chalk, then painted over with an artist's brush. To create a more pristine pattern, use scroll stencils.

77

78

GINGHAM CHECKS Add

designer style to your walls with a paint finish inspired by a favorite American fabric: gingham. A squeegee with ½-inch notches was used to apply the lavender pattern on the white wall *above*. For a softer look, try painting the wall with two shades of the same color, such as dark gray over medium gray, or medium green over light green.

79

SOFT STRIPES Create depth in a

windowless space by adding lighter stripes to an already painted wall. In the loft at *left*, 10-inch-wide stripes were applied with a wool painter's mitt to lighten the medium-blue textured walls.

80 DIAMONDS

Add sparkle to your walls by creating a harlequin pattern. Base-coat the walls and let dry. Tape off a large diamond pattern (ours uses 14-inch squares placed diagonally). Apply paint with a kitchen sponge to every other diamond. For a softer washed effect, mix paint with glaze—available at paint stores and home centers—before applying the color. Finish by stenciling on tulips.

on ne badine pas avec l'amour
la beauté est une logique perçue comme un plaisir.
la beauté n'est que la promesse du bonheur.
la mesure de l'amour, c'est d'aimer sans mesure
ces plaisirs qu'on nomme, à la légère, physiques
ce qui est beau est moral, voilà tout et rien de plus...
est-ce-que j'ai une gueule d'atmosphère
le temps est un chien qui ne mord que les pauvres.

Bath Splash

GIVE YOUR BATH A SMART NEW LOOK IN A WEEKEND'S TIME BY UPDATING THE WALLS, THE FLOORING, OR THE COUNTERTOPS.

For soothing style, splash walls with a translucent glaze of pale yellow or soft taupe, then accentuate the mirror or the medicine cabinet frame with a stenciled border. Increase privacy by installing a new glass-block window. Give your countertops and floors a fresh look by coating existing surfaces with paint or installing new tiles. Complete your update by accessorizing with personalized towels. For easy-to-follow directions, see pages 95–96.

81-83

SURFACE STYLE

Revive your bath with one of the three ideas shown *opposite:* (81) Soften and shine walls with a coat of tinted glaze. (82) Use stencils or draw freehand script borders with a paint marker to accentuate a round mirror and add interest to walls. (83) Unite a suite with color. This bath shares a palette with the adjoining bedroom.

84-86

PAINT PERFECTION
Keep costs down and style high by updating your bath's surfaces with paint, as shown *above* and *opposite*. **(84)** Coat a worn vinyl floor with heavy-duty paint applied in a checkerboard pattern. **(85)** Paint a dated vanity countertop cream, then add attractive diamond-shape accents. **(86)** Keep the pattern going by updating the walls with tone-on-tone harlequin diamonds. For instructions on how to paint walls decoratively, see pages 94-95.

MOLDING MAKEOVER These penny-wise
accents *above* and *left* make a bath look like a million bucks: **(87)** Use picture-
frame molding to accent your existing wall mirror, or replace a plain mirror with a
new framed one. **(88)** Encompass the room with chair-rail molding, then cap it
with a narrow shelf. If you want to display collectibles, use 3- or 4-inch-wide
units. **(89)** Add open shelves above the chair rail to increase storage and display
space. **(90)** Install ceiling molding to draw the eye up and create a greater sense
of spaciousness.

87-90

MATERIAL MATTERS
If you have a little more time, replace worn or dated materials with home-center buys, as shown *above* and *opposite*. **(91)** Cover the walls with beaded board: Attach the paneling pieces to wall studs with carpenter nails, then prime and paint the beaded board white for a cottage look. **(92)** Tile the tub surround and the bath floor with stone-look ceramic tiles; for added interest, use different sizes of tile for the walls and the floor. Choose dark grout to add lively contrast while disguising stains. **(93)** Replace a plain glass window with glass block; choose a small-scale pattern to maximize privacy while still admitting lots of natural light. **(94)** Increase storage space by installing a mirrored medicine cabinet between the wall studs.

Furniture Fix-Ups

TRANSFORM FURNITURE INTO FOCAL POINTS WITH AN UNCONVENTIONAL MIXTURE OF SHAPE, TEXTURE, AND PATTERN. Useful yet out-of-the-ordinary furnishings make a decorating statement: "I dare to be different." Here are a few ways to accomplish the dare: Use ropes and tassels as decorative drawer pulls, or update a sideboard with leather and tacks. Replace old cane chair backs with decorative metals typically used for radiator covers. Paint and reupholster your dining chairs so that each is different. Want an even easier idea? Stack a small dresser on top of a larger one and paint them the same color to increase storage space without making the room look crowded. For easy-to-follow directions on how to fix up furniture, see page 97.

ROPE CHEST Routed designs on the drawers, as well as drawer pulls made from decorative rope and tassels, give an old chest of drawers standout style.

95

METAL-BACK CHAIRS Patterned 96

sheet metal designed to conceal radiators replaced the damaged
cane backing in this yard-sale find. The cushion was re-covered with white imitation
suede to create an attractive easy-care finish. Bright blue paint completes the makeover.

98
STACKED DRESSERS

Create a modern version of a traditional chest-on-chest by stacking two chests of drawers of similar styles and painting them to match, as *above*. You'll increase your storage without taking up any extra floor space. For safety's sake, securely bolt the chests together, then attach them to wall studs with wood screws.

97
FABRIC-PANELED ARMOIRE
Instead of putting traditional glass doors on your audio-visual armoire, disguise the equipment with fabric panels. These are made by covering two pieces of plywood with ¼-inch foam padding and then stapling fabric to the padded front. Narrow picture-frame molding covers the side seams. The panels slide into the armoire when opened so they don't obstruct viewing.

99

LEATHER-TOPPED SIDEBOARD

Turn a salvaged sideboard into a handsome hunt-style chest by covering the wood with a mixture of paint and glaze, then adorning the top and drawer fronts with fine leather. Applying a strip of tacks by the yard provides a fail-safe way to perfectly align the trim.

100 INDIVIDUAL CHAIRS Bring an extra burst of color to the breakfast table by painting each chair a different color. For an added twist, cover the seat cushions with a large-scale print attached horizontally, vertically, and on the bias. To give these chairs a timeworn look, the new paint was sanded off in spots that might naturally wear over time. Cushion covers were made from bargain-priced fabric remnants.

Project Instructions

Easy Ottomans

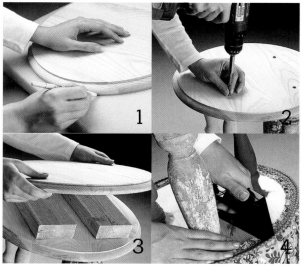

PRETTY PASTELS

Each of these ottomans begins with a base made of two wood layers. Use either 15-inch round pieces or 15-inch square pieces. (If you don't have a power saw, ask a home center to cut plywood for you.) **1.** Trace the wood shape onto 3-inch-thick foam; cut out. **2.** Screw legs to one wood piece. (We used new and vintage balusters for legs.) **3.** Sandwich two 2×4s between the two base pieces; secure with screws to form the ottoman base. Use spray adhesive to secure foam to wood and batting to foam. **4.** Wrap fabric covers, sewn as described below, around the base; staple fabric to bottom, clipping and overlapping where necessary for a smooth fit.

WHAT YOU'LL NEED:

- Padded wooden ottoman base (see above)
- Assorted vintage tablecloths, or new calico or checked fabrics
- Piping cord
- Batting (optional)
- 3-inch-diameter button and covering kit (optional)
- Decorative trim (optional, we used pom-pom fringe)
- Fabric glue (optional)
- Staple gun and staples
- Carpet thread (optional)

TO FINISH A ROUND OTTOMAN: Cut a 16-inch-diameter circle of fabric for the top and a 6×96-inch strip for the side, piecing as necessary. Gather each long edge of strip to fit around base. Cover piping cord, following instructions below. Sew piping to one gathered edge of the strip. Sew raw edge of the gathered strip to the fabric circle, sandwiching piping in between. Sew ends of strip together; turn right side out.

Slip fabric cover over padded base. Wrap extra fabric under wood base; staple.

If desired, make a matching round cushion by cutting two 16-inch-diameter fabric circles. Sew circles together, sandwiching piping in between and leaving an opening for turning. Clip seam. Turn right side out. Insert batting; sew opening closed. Tuft center of cushion with covered button.

TO FINISH A SQUARE OTTOMAN: Cut a 27 inch square from fabric; wrap around padded base, mitering corners. Staple extra fabric to bottom, clipping for a smooth fit. Glue decorative trim or piping to finished bottom edge of base.

If desired, make a second square cushion by cutting one 15-inch square foam piece, two 16-inch square fabric pieces, and four 4×16-inch side strips. Cover piping cord with contrasting fabric.

Sew short ends of side strips together, then sew to a square, sandwiching piping in between. Sew on remaining square, sandwiching piping in between and leaving an opening for turning. Trim corners. Turn right side out. Insert cushion. Sew opening closed. Hand-sew cushion to base with carpet thread.

TO COVER PIPING CORD: Use a straightedge and marking pen to mark strips of contrasting fabrics that are 1–2 inches wide. Cut enough strips of fabric to cover the piping cord. As an alternative, use matching fabric, cutting strips on the bias. Sew cut strips end to end to make one or more long strips. Press seam allowances open and trim edges. Place the long strip facedown; lay piping cord down the center of the strip. Fold the strip in half over the cord; baste. Use a zipper foot to sew right next to the cord. Sew the piping to the right side of the project with the raw edges aligned.

SIMPLE SLIPS

Slip this soft, colorful cover *below* over any old ottoman for a summery touch.

WHAT YOU'LL NEED:

- Ottoman to cover
- Sheer floral fabric for cover
- Complementary sheer checked fabric for corner insets and ties
- Sheer ribbon (optional)
- Matching threads

Sew with right sides together and use ½-inch seam allowances unless otherwise specified.

Size the project to fit the ottoman; for each fabric piece, add 1 inch all around for seam allowances. Measure the length and width of the ottoman top; cut piece from sheer floral fabric. Measure width and height of each side of ottoman; cut pieces from floral sheer fabric. Pin floral pieces together as shown *below* and sew using 1-inch seam allowances. Cut seam allowances to ¼ inch; zigzag-stitch to finish.

Lay slipcover flat on a work surface. Cut four squares of checked sheer fabric to fit corners, adding ½-inch seam allowances. Cut eight 18-inch lengths of sheer ribbon, or make ties

Simple Slipcovers

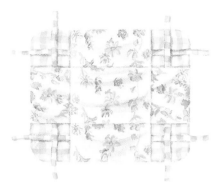

from the checked fabric. Cut one end of each ribbon diagonally, and seal edge by searing it with a lighted match. (Practice on a scrap first.)

Sew squares and ribbons into corners, sandwiching ribbons between fabric layers. Round off the edge of each corner square, as shown. Press all edges under ½ inch; press under an additional ½ inch, and sew hem.

NO-FUSS CUBES

Felt squares and foam make these block-shape ottomans fast and fun.

WHAT YOU'LL NEED:

- ½ yard each of 45- to 72-inch wide felt in three colors
- Three 15-inch squares of 5-inch-thick foam*
- Extra-loft batting
- Spray upholstery glue
- #5 black pearl cotton for trim

Look for extra-thick foam at an auto upholstery supply store or special-order it from a fabrics or crafts store.

Glue three layers of foam together to make a 15-inch-high cube. Glue batting to all sides of foam. Cut six squares of felt—two from each of the three colors. With wrong sides facing and using ¼-inch seam allowances, stitch four sides together to form a cube. Stitch top to cube. Stitch to one side of cube bottom. Insert foam; baste closed. For decorative seam, work pearl cotton running stitches along each seam.

Sew all slipcovers using ½-inch seam allowances and with right sides together, unless otherwise noted.

NAPKIN COVER-UP

Made of two colorful cloth napkins, this seat cover can be made in minutes.

WHAT YOU'LL NEED:

- 20-inch square cloth napkins (two for each chair cover)
- 3 yards ½-inch-wide flat trim
- High-loft batting
- 27-inch-long braiding with tassels
- Fabric marking pen

Stitch gold trim along edges of one napkin. Place a napkin on the chair diagonally, right side up, positioning the corners until you achieve the desired look. With the napkin still on the chair, mark an outline of the chair seat onto the napkin using a fabric marking pen.

Measure the depth and the width of the chair seat and use these measurements to cut a layer of batting; pin the batting to the wrong side of the marked napkin, within the outline. Pin napkins wrong sides together with the batting sandwiched in between. Stitch on the marked line.

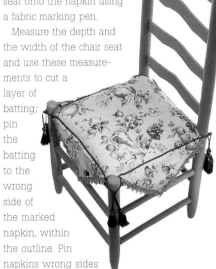

To finish, center braiding along each side seam so the tassels hang evenly from the corners. Zigzag-stitch over ties. Place chair cover on chair and tie with tasseled ends.

FLIRTY SKIRT

Use a short skirt like the one *below* to show off a chair with great shape.

WHAT YOU'LL NEED:

- Medium-weight fabric for seat cushion and skirt
- Contrasting fabric for trim
- Lightweight floral wire
- Acrylic paint
- Paintbrush
- Clear polyurethane
- Newsprint for making slipcover pattern

To lighten the overall look of the chair without making it appear brand-new, rub white acrylic paint on the chair frame, then wipe it off in places that often receive wear. Apply two coats of clear polyurethane to protect the finish.

Lay the newsprint on the chair seat and trace around the edges. Repeat the process for the chair apron. The apron shown is 5 inches long. Allow 20 inches of extra fabric for standard box pleats. Add ½-inch seam allowances all around and cut out the patterns. Cut two fabric pieces for each pattern. Sew together seat top and bottom, leaving an opening for turning.

Cut trim fabric on the bias and sew it to the skirt. Also make ribbon ties from the contrasting fabric. To give the skirt and bows their shape, slip lightweight floral wire between the fabric layers before sewing them together. Fashion the skirt into a standard box-pleat design. Turn seat cushion and stitch skirt to seat at inside edge. If desired, sew piping and chair ties to right side. Place a loose foam pad on the seat beneath the skirt to add softness.

Simple Slipcovers

CHAIR CAPS

These sheer chair caps measure 13 inches long, including a 4-inch band of coordinating fabric.

WHAT YOU'LL NEED:
• Sheer fabric
• Contrasting fabric for trim band
• Newsprint for creating cap pattern

Lay the chair back on the floor atop newsprint. Mark the middle of the chair back on the paper and trace around the edges of the back to the desired length. Subtract 4 inches from length for coordinating band. Add ½-inch seam allowances all around and cut out the pattern. Pin pattern to two layers of fabric; cut out. To determine the width of the boxing strip joining the cap front and back, measure thickness of the chair back, being generous for ease. For length, measure the distance around the cap. Add 1 inch to measurements. Cut out boxing strip. Pin front of chair cap to boxing strip; sew. Stitch back to boxing strip.

For a decorative band, measure around the bottom edge of the cap; cut a 9-inch-wide piece of coordinating sheer to this measurement. With wrong sides together, press the band in half lengthwise. Sew band to bottom edge of cap; sew ends of band together.

CHAIR DRAPE AND RUNNER

These instructions call for gluing, but you may stitch the hems and attach the rickrack and ties with machine sewing if desired.

WHAT YOU'LL NEED:
• Purchased tablecloth, 60×84 inches
• Fabric paint
• Fabric stamps (we used three leaf shapes)

• Cosmetic sponges
• Artist's brushes
• Fabric glue
• Buttons
• 10 yards jumbo white rickrack
• 4 yards twill tape
• Two tassels

Wash and dry the tablecloth to remove the sizing. Do not use fabric softener. Press the fabric and lay it flat. Add 3 inches to the length and width measurements of the chairs to be covered. Cut the fabric along the two long edges of the tablecloth for the chair covers; use the remaining fabric for the table runner. Use any leftover fabric for napkins.

Fold under and press ½ inch on all unfinished edges. Then fold under and press 1¼ inches along the long edges of the chair covers and ½ inch along the table runner edges. (Do not fold the ends into points yet.) Secure hems with a thin line of glue using the pointed end of the applicator. Let the glue dry.

Practice stamping on paper first. Then lay the fabric over a firm surface and tape it in place. To stamp the design, dip a cosmetic sponge into paint. Use the corner of the sponge to apply paint to small areas of the stamp, using a blotting motion and smoothing the color with long strokes if necessary. Press the stamp firmly and evenly onto the fabric. Remove the stamp by lifting it straight off the fabric. Reload

the stamp and continue. If paint builds up on the stamp, rinse it with water, pat it dry with paper towels, and reapply the paint. If the stamped image isn't solid, fill in the design with a brush.

For additional decoration, outline the leaves with a complementary-color acrylic paint, then add swirls and dots. Let the paint dry overnight. Do not wash the fabrics for at least 72 hours. Hand-wash the fabrics in warm water and hang to dry.

Fold the corners of the table runner to the back to create points. Glue the edges in place. Glue rickrack along the edges of the runner and chair covers, wrapping the ends to the back. Glue or hand-sew the ties and buttons to the chair covers; add the tassels to the pointed ends of the table runner.

CLASSIC COVER-UP

This full-length slipcover shows off a chair's shape while covering its flaws. Choose a simple, classic material, such as ticking. For a more tailored look, add piping around the seat cover. Special accents, such as bows and back pleats, can also dress up the look.

WHAT YOU'LL NEED:
• Medium-weight fabric
• Contrasting fabric for piping
• Newsprint for creating pattern
• Lightweight florist's wire
• Hook-and-loop tape

Lay the chair back on the floor atop newsprint. Mark the middle of the chair back on the paper and trace around the edges of the back to the desired length. Also trace seat and determine measurements for apron. Add ½-inch seam allowances all around and cut out the patterns. Pin patterns to two layers of fabric; cut out, allowing for thickness of the chair back and being generous for ease.

Sew cut pieces and piping together to create the look shown on *page 43*. Use hook-and-loop fastening tape to close the cover at the back seam; it encourages a forgiving and wrinkle-free fit that's less likely to shift.

Wonderful Walls

For all projects, tape off baseboards and crown moldings to protect them from paint. Cover floors with drop cloths.

FLOWER FIELDS OR SCROLLS

WHAT YOU'LL NEED:
- Latex paint in two or three shades
- Flower or scroll stencil
- Small sponge roller
- Paint tray
- Stencil adhesive

Paint the walls with two coats of same-color latex paint; let dry. Lightly spray the stencil with stencil adhesive, and position it at the top of the wall. Evenly load the sponge roller with complementary-color paint and roll it over the stencil openings *(photo 1)*.

Carefully lift off the stencil. Reposition the stencil to the right of the completed design, overlapping the last column of the first stencil to line up the design for even spacing. Repeat to stencil a full field of flowers or scrolls. Let the paint dry.

If using a two-layer stencil, spray the detail stencil with stencil adhesive and use the registration marks to align the top and bottom flower pattern. Press the stencil onto the wall. Load the stencil with a second shade *(photo 2)*, repositioning as needed to complete the details on all the stencils.

WALL ART

WHAT YOU'LL NEED:
- Latex paint in six colors
- Leaf stamp
- #10 artist's brush
- 1-inch sponge brush
- Paint tray
- Colored pencil or chalk
- Low-tack painter's tape
- Level and ruler

Using a level and a colored pencil, divide the walls into upper and lower portions. (The 7-inch leaf border will separate these.) Apply painter's tape next to the line. Firmly press the tape to the wall with your fingers or the edge of a plastic card to prevent paint from seeping under the tape. Paint the upper portion of the wall the desired shade, covering the pencil line with paint. Remove the painter's tape and let the paint dry.

Tape off the lower portion of the wall with painter's tape and paint it another color. Remove the tape and let the paint dry. Tape off and paint the narrowest stripes along the upper and lower edges of the border. Let the paint dry. Tape off and paint the 5-inch border with a contrasting color. Remove the tape and let the paint dry.

To create the leaf design, apply the darkest shade of paint to the stamp with the sponge brush using a blotting motion. Experiment with the amount of paint on the stamp by first stamping the design on paper. Too little paint on the stamp results in a faint image; too much paint may cause the stamp to slide and mar the image.

Using the photograph on *page 74* as a guide, firmly and evenly press the stamp to the wall.

Lift the stamp straight off the surface. Reload the stamp and repeat process along the border. Touch up with the artist's brush, as needed.

Determine placement and dimension of the painted frames according to the size of your artwork. The inner borders on *page 74* extend 4 inches from the print-frame edges; the outer borders are 1 inch wide. The painted borders are approximately 8 inches apart. The distance between the lower edge of the painted frames and the leaf border is approximately 30 inches.

GINGHAM CHECKS

WHAT YOU'LL NEED:
- Semigloss acrylic paint
- Wall glaze
- Paint tray and roller
- Low-tack painter's tape
- Paintbrush
- Squeegee with ½-inch notches
- Clean, damp rags

Because of its strong pattern, this technique works best under a chair rail or on a small section of the room. Try other color combinations, such as red and white, for bolder style. Don't worry if your technique isn't perfect—subtle flaws add to the charm.

Base-coat walls with the lightest paint; let dry. Tape off a 4-foot-square section of wall and any moldings. Mix 5 parts glaze with 1 part top-coat paint. Roll glaze mixture on the section *(photo 1, opposite)*. Fill in edges using a paintbrush *(photo 2)*.

While glaze is still wet, start at the top of the section and pull squeegee down the wall to make vertical stripes *(photo 3)*. Wipe off squeegee with a damp rag. Repeat across the section, working quickly. Immediately pull the squeegee left to right to make horizontal stripes, starting at the top of the wall *(photo 4)*. Remove painter's tape.

Repeat across the wall in 4-foot-wide sections, working over the wet edge in each adjacent section.

Wonderful Walls

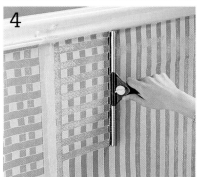

DIAMONDS OR SOFT STRIPES

WHAT YOU'LL NEED:

- Calculator
- Latex paint in two shades (more if you add a stenciled or stamped pattern)
- Paintbrush
- Synthetic kitchen sponges
- 1-inch sponge brush
- Chalk line
- Low-tack painter's tape
- Level, carpenter's square, and ruler

FOR DIAMONDS: Use a calculator to figure out the best size diamonds for your room. For large-scale patterns, set aside a weekend to paint a 10×12 foot room. The smaller the pattern, the more time required to complete the project. Brush on a base coat in one of the colors of your diamond pattern.

After the base coat dries, plot the diamond pattern with a partner: Across the top and bottom of each wall, measure and mark the width of each diamond. (For example, for a 2-foot-wide diamond, make pencil marks at 2-foot intervals.) Along each side of the wall, mark the diamond height. (For example, for 4-foot-high diamonds, make pencil marks at 4-foot intervals.) Stretch and snap chalk lines on the marks to create the grid. Use a carpenter's square and level to check your work as you progress.

Use synthetic kitchen sponges to apply paint. A damp sponge with square corners works to define the diamond edges. Use a second, larger damp sponge to fill in the diamond color, and a third to wipe off some of the color to achieve the degree of mottling that you want.

If desired, follow the stenciling or stamping directions on *pages 93–94* to layer on an additional motif, such as the tulips *below*.

FOR STRIPES: Follow the instructions for the diamonds, except mark off stripes with paint. Use a sponge or a painter's mitt to apply paint to every other stripe. Experiment with a mixture of glaze and paint to create the washed effect you prefer.

Bath Splash

INSTALL GLASS-BLOCK PANEL

Bathrooms in many older homes have windows in the tub area, creating a privacy issue. Consider replacing a window with a panel of glass block as shown in the bath on *page 84*. You can buy preformed panels in limited sizes or build one yourself, allowing the mortar to cure as recommended by the manufacturer.

Remove parting stops from the window jams to free the sash. Interior casing (the trim surrounding the window frame) can remain in some cases. Remove the sash and any cords, weights, or pulleys.

Place tapered wood shims on the windowsill, and set the glass-block panel in place from the inside. If exterior trim or stops on the old window frame won't prevent the glass-block assembly from falling through the opening, fasten a couple of temporary stops in place. Adjust the wood sill shims to level the block assembly, then place shims at the top and sides to secure it. Make sure the face of the glass-block panel is flush with the inside edge of the window frame for fitting wood or tile trim later. Spray expanding-foam insulation to seal the space between the panel and the window frame; let dry. Trim the excess foam with a utility knife. Working from the outside of the window, fill the bottom gap (between the windowsill and glass block) with mortar; let set for 15–30 minutes, then remove the wood shims and plug those gaps with mortar. Cut and fit cedar 1×4-inch stock as trim around the sides and top of the window exterior. Secure the cedar with 6d galvanized finishing nails.

Caulk all edges where the cedar trim meets the glass and window frame. Prime and paint all exposed wood surfaces, including mortar joints between blocks if desired.

Bath Splash

TILE A FLOOR

Careful measurement and preparation are key when tiling a floor.

Remove old flooring down to the subfloor. Attach cement board to the subfloor with screws. Measure the width of the floor, halve that number, and pencil a line at that point across the floor. Repeat the process to find the halfway point of the room's length, and pencil a mark across the floor from wall to wall. (You'll end up with two lines that intersect at the room's center.)

Before applying adhesive, place the corner of the first tile at the point where the penciled lines intersect, then center other tiles consecutively along the line, leaving about ⅛ inch between the tiles for grout lines. Arrange the tiles so the least amount of cutting is necessary. Mark their locations with a pencil, then remove them. Apply adhesive, such as mastic, to a 3-foot section with the notched trowel recommended by the adhesive manufacturer (photo 1).

Following the pencil marks, lay the first tile in the adhesive. Use temporary spacers for even grout lines. Continue laying tile (photo 2) until you get to the walls; cut remaining tiles with a scorer to fit. If you need to tile around pipes or other items, use tile nippers or consider renting a wet saw to make cutting and shaping tiles easier. Let the adhesive dry as recommended by the manufacturer.

Remove the spacers with needle-nose pliers, then apply grout with a float (photo 3). Let the grout dry for the time recommended by the manufacturer, usually 15 minutes. With a damp sponge, wipe the grout residue from the faces of the tiles (photo 4). Rinse the sponge frequently and wipe the tiles until all residue is removed. Let the grout dry as recommended by the manufacturer.

PAINT A LAMINATE COUNTER

Preparation, paint, and proper sealing are the keys to painting a laminate countertop that offers lasting looks.

Clean the surface as you normally would. Protect what you don't want to paint with tape or drop cloths.

Choose primer (Zinsser BIN, an alcohol-base primer, was used on the counter below right). Ask the paint store to tint the primer the same color as the base paint. Brush or roll on the primer; let dry according to manufacturer's directions. Roll or brush on the base coat; let dry.

Draw your design on the countertop. (The countertop in the featured bath on page 81 has a taupe square on either side of the sink.) Tape off areas of the design that will be a different color from your base coat, then roll or brush on paint. Let dry; remove tape.

For lettering, such as "his" and "hers" labels, either stencil the letters onto the countertop, or draw the words on black artist's paper (available at art supply stores) and cut out each letter with a crafts knife. Mount the letters onto the counter with spray adhesive. The latter option is best for a less-trafficked room, such as a guest bath.

Protect your design with three or four coats of polyurethane, letting dry between coats.

PAINT A VINYL FLOOR

Plan a design for the floor. (A square pattern in cream and taupe with black accent diamonds adorns the floor on page 80.) Choose latex or oil-base paints that will adhere to primer (read the primer's label to be sure).

Painting a vinyl floor requires meticulous surface preparation. Glue down any rips or loose areas of vinyl. Clean the floor as usual; let dry. Sand lightly with sandpaper or a hand-sander (depending on square footage) to rough up the surface so the primer and paint will adhere.

Choose a heavy-duty surface primer. Have the store tint the primer to match the base paint color. Protect the surfaces you don't want to paint with drop cloths or tape. Roll primer onto the floor, starting in a corner opposite the doorway. Let dry according to the manufacturer's directions. (Note: Primer will help level the floor surface, even if the vinyl is lightly textured.) Using a roller, apply the base paint to the entire floor; let it dry according to the label's instructions.

Mark the chosen design on the floor using a yardstick and a pencil; tape off the areas that will be a different color from the base coat. Use a brush for an intricate design or a roller for large-scale work to apply the contrasting paint color. Let dry; remove tape. Repeat for other colors or design layers as necessary.

When the design is complete, roll on three or four coats of polyurethane, letting it dry after each coat.

EMBELLISH A TOWEL

To add details to plain terry-cloth towels, below right, purchase pom-pom trim and rickrack from a fabrics store. Attach the decorative trim using snaps sewn to the trim and the towel; that way, the trim can be removed when you machine-wash the towels.

Furniture Fix-Ups

METAL-BACK CHAIR

WHAT YOU'LL NEED:
- Old cane-back chair
- Patterned sheet metal
- Tin snips
- Tape measure
- Leather work gloves
- Staple guns and staples
- Primer
- High-gloss latex paint

Reincarnate an old cane-back chair by removing the cane, priming, and painting the chair. (We used a high-gloss bright blue paint.) For the new back, use patterned sheet metal designed to conceal radiators (available at home centers). Measure and mark the sheet metal to fit, adding ¼ inch all the way around to fit the existing rabbet. Wearing work gloves, cut the metal with tin snips. Staple the back in place in the rabbet as shown *below;* use a screwdriver to bend the raw edges back into the existing caning groove.

ROPE CHEST

WHAT YOU'LL NEED:
- Unfinished or old chest
- Lint-free cloths
- Water-base wood stain
- Black latex paint
- Polyurethane
- Upholstery string
- Washers or buttons
- Decorative rope and tassels
- Chalk
- Craft tool with sanding and wood-carving bits

Remove hardware and drawers. If necessary, strip off the finish. Using a craft tool equipped with wood-carving and sanding bits, practice carving a pattern on scrap wood. When you're ready, draw a pattern on the drawers with chalk and carve with a steady hand using the carving bit. Clean up the carved pattern with the sanding bit. With a lint-free cloth, rub desired stain over the chest.

For instant age, water down black paint, and use a cloth to rub the thinned color around the edges of the chest. Protect the finish with two coats of polyurethane; let dry.

Embellish each drawer with a pair of tassels linked by a long decorative rope. Secure tassels to the drawer by threading upholstery string through each tassel and through the existing hardware holes in the drawers. Inside the drawer, prevent the string from pulling back through by securing the end with a washer or button.

STACKED DRESSERS

Stacked chests will be more secure if the top chest is smaller.

WHAT YOU'LL NEED:
- Two similar chests, one smaller than the other
- White paint and polyurethane
- Matching knobs
- Fine-grit sandpaper
- Lint-free cloths
- Paintbrush
- Screws, bolts, and washers

Remove the legs from the top chest, if necessary. Remove the drawers and hardware from both chests. Sand pieces, then wipe them clean with a damp cloth. Prime and paint both chests and drawers with two coats of white paint; let dry. Apply two coats of polyurethane; let dry. Install new knobs and slip drawers into chests. Stack smaller chest on top of larger chest. Attach chests together with wood screws, bolts, and washers as needed. Attach top chest to wall studs.

LEATHER-TOPPED SIDEBOARD

WHAT YOU'LL NEED:
- Unfinished or salvaged sideboard
- Sandpaper
- Latex primer
- Latex paint
- Colored glaze
- Sea sponge
- Polyurethane
- Decorative upholstery tacks
- Leather
- Staple gun and staples

Remove hardware and drawers if necessary; sand, clean, and prime the sideboard. Apply two coats of paint (we used burnt orange); let dry. Apply a light coating of glaze (we used a dark coffee color) using a sea sponge and a soft dabbing motion to create the pattern as shown; let dry. Apply two coats of polyurethane; let dry.

Cut leather to cover the top, allowing for foldover. Cut additional leather pieces to fit inside recessed panels on drawer fronts. Pull leather taut and secure in place on underside of top and at corners of recessed panels with a staple gun and staples. Push decorative tacks in place using the photo *above* as a guide.

Big Style,
Small Rooms

We want to show you 100 ways to make your small spaces live larger so your rooms are rich with style. It's amazing the difference that turning a chair slightly, adding a mirror, or painting a wall can make—all without breaking the bank.

In the living room chapter, *pages 128–153*, you'll find clever built-ins and floor treatments that make a room appear to grow larger before your eyes. We'll show you the striking impact of wall texture and how well-placed large-scale items create a showstopping space.

In the bedroom chapter, *pages 100–117*, we'll teach you a few storage tricks to reduce clutter while making room for artwork and keepsakes that bring out your personal style. And see how easy, everyday decorating ideas, such as sassy window treatments, create focal points.

We didn't forget about the hub of the home. Getting the most out of your kitchen is a snap if you follow the examples on *pages 154–169*. Divide a space with an island, employ fold-away furniture, and turn nifty nooks into spaces that serve dual purposes.

In this section, you'll also find chapters focusing on found spaces, home offices, and the art of furniture arranging. We hope this collection helps you create a home you'll love.

Relaxation Quarters

The bedroom is the last place you see before you fall asleep and the first place to greet you upon waking. More than any other room in the house, it is your personal sanctuary, a place you trust to keep you safe until morning. Decorate it with soothing colors, dramatic window treatments, and treasured mementos from family and friends. Where space is limited, find display solutions for photographs, such as a shelf above a headboard or a dresser at the end of your bed. And be sure to look for smart storage ideas that enhance your style while hiding clothes and other personal items.

double trouble

A built-in sleeping berth can turn an ordinary bedroom into an exotic getaway. This small room *opposite* has unique space for two because bunk beds are tucked under an ogee arch. The recessed beds provide another benefit: free floor space.

02

the sky's the limit

Add height to a room with a tall headboard. This built-in headboard frees up floor space and doubles as a spot for showing off mementos. Its vertical lines, combined with the thick stripes on the wall, lead the eye upward. Thinner stripes above the headboard continue around the room to complete the look.

far-reaching light

Don't waste bedside table space on a lamp—install wall-mounted lights. Swivel arms on a bedside lamp make for easy reading whether you're sitting or lying down.

03

Find storage in hidden places to free up

tucked **under**

Say good-bye to dust bunnies with built-in under-bed storage.
These drawers are easy to access and complement the
furniture's sleek design.

04

table surfaces for other bedside essentials.

05

clean and simple

Sure it's a decorative element, but this
bed skirt also has a practical purpose:
It hides pullout drawers. A storage
chest at the end of the bed holds
laundry and provides extra seating.

06

instant closet

Use curtains to create a closet. When this room was
converted into a bedroom, wire storage pieces were
anchored to the wall to create a needed closet.
Ceiling-hung curtains wrap around the unit to
conceal the contents from view.

07

clear
height

These sheer panels create long lines when suspended from the ceiling on decorative iron hooks instead of from above the window frame on an ordinary curtain rod.

08

room
with a view

Devise a sense of openness by framing a stunning view. Positioning the bed directly in front of the window takes full advantage of the vine outside this bedroom. Dramatic red toile curtains put the window and bed in focus.

Bolts of luxurious fabric turn windows into focal points.

09 break away

Make a room look active by pulling furniture away from the walls, even in a tight space. Angled from a corner, this colorfully clothed twin bed lends interest to the room. Wild stripes add a feeling of height to the small bedroom, and a wooden cabinet with a lattice front decoratively hides a heating unit.

10 compact comfort

You don't need a grand space to have grand comfort. Built-in storage leaves floor space for a wing chair. A desk tucked into an alcove takes in the view from a window.

11 bed end

Forget about a footboard. Tuck a chest at the foot of a bed. This one gives the bed a finished look and provides valuable storage space for bulky clothes or blankets.

nifty shelves

Personalize shelves with knickknacks. Packed with books, collectibles, and plants, these built-in bookshelves create a cozy, lived-in feel that matches the earthy tone of the exposed ceiling.

12

13

let in light

With an ocean view, this attic was too valuable to sit unused. Skylights open up the space, and built-in storage shelves help keep the bedroom's lines simple.

14

sweeping lines

Take advantage of architectural features. This slanted room provided the perfect opportunity to create a storybook bedroom. Combined with nostalgic furnishings, the gentle flowing canopy creates a fairy-tale feel.

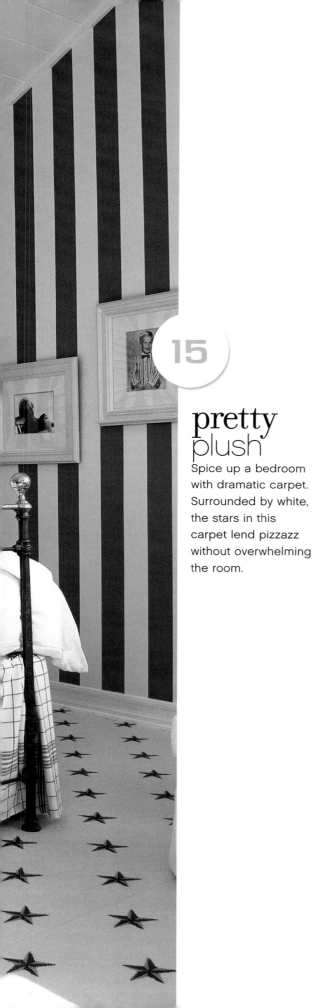

on display

Position a desk or chest at the foot of a bed to use its surface space for an organized display. Show off favorite portraits in coordinating frames that work with the room's decor.

16

15

pretty plush

Spice up a bedroom with dramatic carpet. Surrounded by white, the stars in this carpet lend pizzazz without overwhelming the room.

17

big can be better

A small space doesn't have to dictate small furniture. In fact, if you use a few large pieces, you can reduce clutter in a room. This entertainment center extends the height of the room while providing subtle storage.

clever swivel

In cramped quarters, this television *far left* is attached to a turntable so it rotates to face the sleeping or living area. When not in use, the cabinet doors keep the look clean by hiding the television from view, *left*.

19 two-in-one

Always use leftover space. In addition to providing tons of organized storage, this walk-in closet takes advantage of a sunny spot by the window with a desk that serves as a vanity.

Bathing Beauties

There's one guarantee with a bathroom—it comes with a mirror. With this fabulous space-enlarging tool, you're already one step along the road of turning a tiny space into a room that is warm and cheery or daring and dramatic. But what other tools can help get the job done? Plain white walls may provide a spacious feeling, but they're boring. Pump up wall texture with glass, corrugated metal, or paint. Trim the tub, window, or sink with decorative fabric. Pay attention to the details: Select light fixtures that make a style statement, and choose faucets with character. If you splurge on something, make it the vanity—it can carry the entire bathroom.

20

guiding light

Substitute glass for plaster. Sunlight streams into this small bathroom *opposite* thanks to an almost floor-to-ceiling wall of translucent glass block. Neutral tile, a simple sink, and a large mirror add elegance without clutter.

21

stamp it

Dress up plain materials with simple paint techniques. The walls, sink skirt, shower curtain, and floor rug in this bathroom were trimmed with a decorative pattern applied with a leaf-motif stamp. Select from a variety of paints to get the job done: Flat latex, glazes, and acrylics work well on different textures.

22

within
reach

Carve out shelving space. This narrow unit keeps reading materials close at hand and provides two ledges on which to set flowers and knickknacks.

23

privacy
screen

Use fabric to ensure privacy. This striped panel stops prying eyes yet still allows a casement window to open. As a whimsical extra, trim the panel with beads or other decorative embellishments.

powder power

Transform a coat closet into a powder room. Just $3\frac{1}{2} \times 2\frac{1}{2}$ feet, this closet still provides enough room for an extra-small sink and a mirror. A silver basket-weave design gives the walls and door a sleek look.

25

24

glowing illusions

Install a light by a mirror. No matter what size room you have, a light paired with a mirror, *above* and *opposite,* creates a reflective synergy that makes wattage go farther, thus enhancing the perceived size of a room.

26

rich color

Add life without creating a closed-in feeling by using a simple, rich color scheme balanced with white. A generous floor-to-ceiling shower curtain and recessed ceiling lights help elongate this tiny bath.

diamonds forever

Update uninspired walls with an engaging finish. Measured, taped, and painted, this diamond pattern turns a weathered bathroom into a lively spectacle. Decorative beads glued to the intersection points provide a playful touch.

27

simple
skirting

28

Relax a bath by removing the door on a vanity in favor of a skirt. This fabric is attached to the sink with hook-and-loop tape. A split in the front provides easy access to toiletries.

29

dual-ing sinks

Rethink space problems, then think again. This bathroom had enough space for a large window or a double-sink vanity, but not both—or so it seemed. Dual sinks standing back-to-back solved the dilemma. A photography studio pole supports a mirror, towel rack, and wastebasket.

30

say it with photos

Simply appointed, this bathroom needed a touch of character. A photo rail was constructed from 1×6 trim board; evenly sized and spaced horizontal cutouts were made. Acrylic plastic panels cover the photos, and a hinged rail cover sits on top to allow easy access.

Gathering Space

A living room is home to the sofa you retreat to after a hard day's work. It's also the first place you take friends when they visit. As the center of relaxation and entertaining, a living room needs to be comfortable enough for a cozy afternoon of reading, yet stylish enough for an elegant dinner party with friends. If you're challenged by a small, boxy space, let light, color, and artwork perform magic. A room may lack square footage, but smart furniture placement and decorative accents in just the right places can trick the eye into thinking a space is larger than its confines.

31

art at work
Sometimes, less is more. A giant framed wall map steals the show in this living room. Its large scale makes a dramatic, eye-catching statement but doesn't let the tight space look busy.

It doesn't take much to turn dead wall

32

circle this

Use artwork to add a sense of movement. A semicircle of plates positioned over a lively rectangular painting stirs things up in this living room *opposite.* The vibrant painting inspired the color scheme for the rest of the room.

33

all lined up

Turn wall space into a visual treat by grouping symmetrical pieces of art. *Above left,* three simple photos stacked vertically transform an awkward space between two windows into a picturesque spot. *Left,* four pictures hung along a wall provide depth and reinforce the room's decorating theme.

space into an artistic showcase.

34

box of **tricks**

Now you see it; now you don't. Ottomans that double as
storage boxes are great as footrests and as table
surfaces in a pinch. They also keep magazines,
blankets, and children's toys hidden but accessible.

35

classy
glass

Lend some relief to a crowded spot with glass-topped furniture. A triangular glass coffee table with softened edges encourages an open and airy feel, even as several pieces of furniture jockey for attention.

36

heat contained

Keep an ugly heater under wraps and gain shelf space with a vent cover. Crafted from wood, this unit blends with the window treatment to turn a distracting room feature into an advantage.

37

table tricks

Choose a flat and sturdy footstool as a living room centerpiece. It can serve as a table, as well as an additional seating option. Covered in a playful plaid fabric, this footstool lends masculinity to the room, balancing the more feminine elements.

38 light my fire

Weave an enchanting spell by spreading light around a room. Well-placed recessed lights accent artwork and provide light without taking up valuable floor space. Supplement recessed lights with a few small lamps for reading.

39 storage showcase

Not all shelving has to be alike. Custom-design a bookcase to fit some of your favorite mementos. Mix up the shelf spacing and add low-voltage lighting under the lip of the shelves to spotlight your showpieces.

40

soaring
heights

High ceilings add another dimension for sprucing up a room. In this living room, green walls frame the view and draw the eye up to a vaulted ceiling, where the architectural angles spotlight a favorite art collection.

41

print
elegance

Keep the color palette simple, but use complementary prints and colors to lend depth to a small room. Tucked into a sunny window nook, this seating area is an attention-grabber, thanks to the blue-and-white toile curtains, the butter-yellow throw pillows on the sofa, and the striped cushions on the formal chairs.

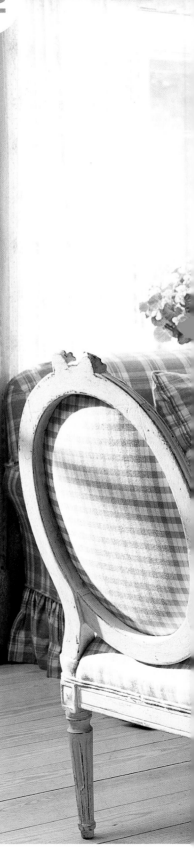

42

in focus

Arrange furniture around a focal point. This lace-dressed bay window immediately captures the eye, but the furniture shares the spotlight in the uncluttered arrangement. Playing on the unexpected, a high tea table stands in for a regular coffee table and serves as a magnificent centerpiece for the Scandinavian-style room.

43

gaining equilibrium

Use furniture to break up a room's boxy shape. Positioned in a circle around a tall tea table, these oversize armchairs make the entrance to this narrow 1880s row house feel spacious. The arrangement also helps direct traffic.

44 elongating lines

Let draperies turn windows into stunning focal points. Small in width, large in height, this living room takes full advantage of the extratall windows by dressing them with luxurious purple-striped, pinch-pleat draperies.

45

color balance

Pick striking wall and molding colors to turn a bland room into an elegant area. Densely sponged over a pale background, the persimmon on this living room's walls picks up the warm tones in the antique rug. The color is a bold backdrop for clean white molding.

46

personal space

Select neutral walls and furniture to increase the size of a small space, then add personal touches to bring out your style. A rug, throw pillows, and a collection of plates bring this room to life. Flower bouquets in vintage vases add flair.

bump it out

Use a bay window to stretch your dimensions. This relaxing alcove offers cozy seating that doesn't steal an inch of floor space.

Build room character by splurging on a piece of furniture you just can't do without.

48

striking
height

Incorporate a tall piece of furniture in a square room. This grandfather clock regally draws the eye upward. A low chair rail also works hard to elongate the room, and sheer draperies add flair while allowing in natural light.

49

basic black

Electronic equipment is no problem for this black-and-white living room. Taking center stage, the television and stereo sit in a clean-lined open cabinet. A bonus: The cabinet top gets a workout as a serving counter in the kitchen.

50

wall unit

Tucked neatly into built-ins, a media center can add drama to a room. Echoing this contemporary home's strong horizontal lines, a long, low grid of shelves is outfitted with books, collectibles, and a television. The combination creates a cohesive focal point.

51

color me happy

Claim a space as your own with your favorite hues. Bold walls, combined with dark molding and neutral furnishings, are all the decoration this living room needs.

52

graceful folds

Go with layers of yardage to create a luxurious look. Puddling on the floor, the draperies feel rich, even though the fabric is light-diffusing cotton.

53

warming effect

Create a snug room by adding texture to the walls. A double-rolling paint technique gives this room multidimensional warmth.

54 in the **dark**

Flanked with freestanding shelving units, this maple armoire becomes an instant focal point. When the doors are closed, you'd never know a fully loaded media center sits inside.

55

built-in drama

Frame a sitting room with shelves. Leaving enough space for a well-appointed Louis XVI daybed, this bookcase creates an intimate seating nook while proudly displaying mementos. Two animal-print lamps provide soft reading light.

56 windows of opportunity

Provide the crowning touch to a room with a window treatment. Make it a decorative accent to a simple room, such as this rod with frills *opposite, top left and top right.* Craft a valance that repeats the color used in your furniture, *opposite, bottom left.* Challenged by a tall, narrow window? Try piecing together panels of fabric, *opposite, bottom right.* Add a sheer center panel to maintain privacy. Or richen a room with an understated lace swag, *above.*

Stirring Up Style

No matter what its size, a kitchen should be useful, organized, and—above all—welcoming. It's a family's communication hub, where meals are made and the day's events discussed. And no one wants to spend time fixing culinary delights in a dark, dingy closet. Make a small kitchen feel larger with a crisp color scheme, and pick appliances that blend in seamlessly. Select cabinetry that's useful on the inside and slimming on the outside. Personalize the space with eye-catching frills, such as lavish window treatments or a checkered floor.

     66

clear possibilities

When viewed through glass-front cabinets, colorful dishes do the decorating. This kitchen may break the small-space design rule of simplicity, but with its funky lamps, colorful dish collections, and a window molding made from picture framing, it oozes character.

dividing
island

67

Use a work island to divide one room into two areas. This island creates the illusion of a wall without blocking light or closing in the spaces. Two pendent fixtures accentuate the division.

68

splashy color

Don't be afraid to go bold when choosing color. This small kitchen was white and blah until shades of red paint, applied in checks, transformed it into a vibrant, energy-filled space.

69

all dressed up

Go retro with a sink skirt. In the 1920s, skirts hid plumbing and provided an attractive cover-up for cleaning supplies. The simple checked fabric adds the perfect touch of country to this kitchen.

70

slick fronts

Employ simple, smooth cabinet fronts to make a small space feel larger. Shake things up by varying cabinet size, shape, and finish.

Punch up a small space with patterned surfaces and bold color.

stow away

Incorporate folding furniture into rooms with limited space. This petite bistro table provides a spot in the kitchen for grabbing a quick bite to eat and offers additional staging space during meal preparation. When not in use, it folds away neatly beside the refrigerator.

Tackle tight spaces by developing design

72

show off your **curves**

Let restaurant-style shelving above a sink provide extra storage. The shelving offers easy access to frequently used dishes, and the elevated counter conceals this kitchen's work areas from the living room.

strategies that reach outside the box.

73

behind
the curtain

A cloth curtain inside a glass cabinet eliminates the appearance of clutter. More eye-catching than a plain cabinet, fabric panels can express your kitchen's style.

a slot for everything

Wrap a refrigerator in storage. Serving platters slip into cubbies on top of this refrigerator, and a wine rack runs down the side. Additional white ceramic pitchers accent the look.

74

75

cover up

Mismatched appliances? No problem. Hide them behind cupboard facades for continuity. The dishwasher in this kitchen sits behind a cabinet door. Custom-made iron pins eliminate the need for door pulls that would ruin the clean lines.

76

a step above the rest

Use changes in floor level to designate entrance into a new space. With no room to spare, this kitchen *below* relies on a raised floor and a decorative treatment to give it prominence. A neat touch: The customized cabinet pulls at *left* were cut from a $14 sheet of aluminum and bent to form ovals.

cabinet refresher 77

Give old cabinets a face-lift with paint. These tired cabinets were given new life with bold blue. A crisp contrast, white trim provides a fresh and open feel.

78

color check

Use checkerboard flooring as a space-expanding solution. This muted green-and-white floor works with earthy green walls to open up this compact kitchen.

79

under foot

Don't forget about floor color. You can dress up a dull floor with hardworking, easy-to-maintain linoleum. This radiant sun design spices up the floor and works with the colorful tiles to jazz up a tight space.

80

window treats

Use window treatments as opportunities to inject color. This white kitchen gains vibrant life from a simple blue-and-white plaid valance. Blue vases and ceramic collectibles subtly reinforce the color introduction.

appliance "garage"

Keep appliances handy but hidden from view. This electrified "garage" houses small kitchen essentials in a condensed space. Behind the door when not in use, the appliances can conveniently be plugged in and slid out when needed.

81

Make every nook and cranny work hard

sit on it

Create secret storage under furniture. No space should go unused, so storage pockets were added to this kitchen's circular dining area. Special-occasion serving pieces hide under cushions.

by performing dual tasks.

ClutterBusters

Look around your home. Is the mail threatening to gobble up the kitchen table? Are important papers stuffed in a shoe box under the bed? Stop fostering clutter and get organized. Whether you work from home or just need an area to track bills and schedules, it's easy to carve out a niche dedicated to controlling the paper piles. Convert a closet into an office, angle a desk to create a room within a room, or simply tuck a disguised filing cabinet into a corner. And remember, hardworking doesn't necessarily mean boring. Splurge on a comfortable chair, hang a picture to create a view, or find storage solutions that do double-duty as decorative elements.

83

closet storage

Transform a closet into a mini office by creating a desk from a wood plank and two filing cabinets. The closet door makes an ideal bulletin board, and built-in shelving provides easy access to a bevy of baskets that hold sorted papers.

84 wall space

A portion of this living room was converted into an efficient wall-to-wall work area. Wicker baskets stashed in cubbies stow files in an attractive fashion, while two large bulletin boards covered with notes and photographs lend personality to the walls.

85

all the right **angles**

Use a desk situated at a right angle to other furniture to subtly create a stylish work area within a room. Furnish the desk with a plush wing chair and situate it near plenty of natural light, and you'll start making up excuses to work.

86

open up

Make a small, dark area feel larger with built-in cubbyholes above a desk. The cubbies preserve openness while fitting the storage bill. Warm up dead wall space with a painting to create a view where there isn't one.

sheer solutions

Let transparent curtains filter the light flooding your office space so you don't have to squint while working. Ever-so-easy to re-create, these sheers are simply two scarves attached to drapery clips and suspended from an ornate iron rod.

88

under wraps

Function isn't always pretty, but you can hide an ugly filing cabinet with a slipcover. Positioned next to a small desk, the filing cabinet creates additional table surface when beautifully disguised.

Clever Nooks

Lurking under the stairs, in the entryway, or inside a closet are spaces that could work harder. Look around your home with fresh eyes. Could you replace a coat tree with snazzy wall hooks? Do you have quirky shelves or window ledges that could host a treasured collection? In homes where space is tight, unused or undecorated niches are wasted opportunities. Get smart. Recast blank walls with room-stretching stripes. Replace a lackluster front door with an ornate one and dress the area in your style. Free up floor space with stackable appliances. One by one, turn leftover nooks into chances to decorate, store, and showcase your favorite things.

stair storage

The area under this open staircase *opposite* could have been nothing more than picture-hanging space, but instead, built-in cabinets with glass panels provide pretty and practical storage.

sweet hooks

90

Choose creative hooks to decorate wall space. These fork hooks *above* are the perfect home for dish towels in a kitchen, and cut-down walking canes, *above right*, give any entry a wonderful country look.

landing upgrade

91

A framed print and small collection of baskets turn this top-of-the-stairs wall space and ledge into a showplace. Guests below now have something to look forward to as they climb.

stack 'em up

Washers and dryers are space hogs. Squeeze them into a tight spot by purchasing stackable units. Now this laundry room has space for shelves and sorting.

92

93

behind closed doors

If the laundry room has to fit into an open floor plan, use an armoire to keep the area tidy. Hang clothes inside the armoire to dry, and use the space to store shoes or other sundry items.

94 entry screen

Many front doors lead straight into the living room. Use a screen, fabric panel, or even a tall bookcase to create an entry.

95

looking glass

Expand an entry by creatively positioning a mirror. Paired with a weathered park bench, this shuttered mirror mimics a window and lends the narrow entryway depth, as well as country flavor.

96

mudroom
magic

Splashy plaid pillows, plenty of coat hooks, and a shelf for shoes turn this mudroom into a destination. Visible from the living room, the mudroom uses an oval window and matching wall color to make the most of the interior view.

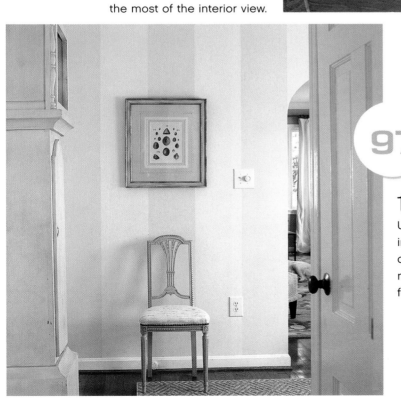

97

tall and wide

Use wide stripes to give an entryway big impact. A grandfather clock, a gilded chair, and a framed print play off the neutral stripes in this entry and provide focal points.

98

wide
passage

Don't overlook the chance to
turn ho-hum hallway space
into something worth looking
at. This wide hallway now
serves as a library, thanks to
built-in bookshelves. Antique
sconces illuminate and
soften the passage.

99

details details

A fanciful door, a colorful floor treatment, and a collection of
antique-framed mirrors turn what could be a drab, almost nonexistent
foyer into an entrance with character and personal flavor, *opposite.*

Blur the line between rooms to create

open, airy, light-diffusing spaces.

100 in the **open**

Keep an open floor plan when possible. Floating behind the yellow supporting columns, this stairway deprives the living room of neither light nor view. Enclosed, the stairway would have split the space and stopped the flow of natural light.

Weekend Walls

Changing the way walls look is one of the most effective ways to freshen a room or give your entire house a new personality. Whether you simply hang a colorful piece of art beside a bookcase or redecorate a whole room with new paint and wallpaper, the effect is immediate and invigorating. But time always seems to be at a premium, so a lot of us are reluctant to jump into a redecorating project.

That's why we gathered this group of our favorite quick and easy ideas to help you add character to one wall or a room in the space of a single weekend. Many of the ideas, such as hanging a grouping of frames or other objects, *pages 206–219*, can be done in a few hours; others will take a day or longer.

Often you can redecorate an entire room working one wall at a time—add a fabric accent to one wall (*pages 246–253*) one weekend, accent another with wallpaper (*pages 254–263*) or a decorative paint treatment (*pages 230–245*) during another. Start with "Rooms with a Hue," *pages 188–205*, which will help you develop an ideal color scheme for your room.

No matter how you decide to approach your project, you're sure to find inspiration and helpful information in this section.

rooms with a hue

Remember **ROY G. BIV**—red, orange, yellow, green, blue, indigo, and violet—the friendly device that helped you learn the **colors of the rainbow** years ago? As an adult looking for ways to give each of the rooms in your house its own **unique feel**, one of the easiest things you can do is bring old Roy to mind again. But with all those **options to choose** from, you'll first have to decide which **hue is right** for **you**.

1

WHITE

There's a reason brides wear white: It's beautiful, elegant, and when employed properly, far from boring. White evokes simplicity and purity; a white bedroom is an especially serene space. And when white walls frame a monochromatic room, the look is white-hot.

So **simple**, yet so striking: White is seen
as a **brilliant color** by the human eye.

2
RED

Think theater curtains: Nothing announces drama better than the color red. Cherry adds regality to a dining space; apple proves more powerful than almost any other hue. And you don't have to go red all over, either. Just one crimson wall is sure to get the attention it deserves.

Like the **red lipstick** you don only
for the most **special occasions,**
crimson walls instantly
infuse a room with attitude.

If you want a room the whole family will love, **let the sunshine in.** Yellow is the first color kids reach for and has a way of **bringing smiles** among young and old alike.

3
YELLOW

When you want to create a room you can really enjoy yourself in, yellow should automatically come to mind. The color practically synonymous with mellow has a midas touch for another reason, too. It brightens up green and pairs perfectly with purple. Even yellow-and-red color schemes earn rave reviews. Whether walls are cream, honey, or lemon, the look is simply delicious.

4
ORANGE

In the '70s, when it worked in cahoots with earth-toned browns and greens, it was a staple. But today, while not called on as often, orange offers an excitement all its own. Known for its vibrancy, orange adds pizzazz to a space, such as a breakfast nook, that could easily be overlooked if not for its fun, sunny walls.

From **celery to forest,** green is not your garden-variety hue. There are more **tints and shades** of green than of any other color.

5

DARK GREENS

Green walls that venture to the dark side do double duty: They impart prestige, making them a good choice for a formal living space, and project a sense of safety and security that's oh-so-necessary for a truly cozy bedroom.

6

LIGHT GREENS

It's only natural: Any room benefits from bringing a little of the outdoors in. Light-toned greens, which work especially well with neutrals like whites, beiges, or grays, are just the hues to do it. Springtime splendor instantly comes to mind in a room with walls reminiscent of enchanting gardens and lush lawns.

7
DARK BLUES

Take a cue from your favorite pair of jeans. Dressing up your walls with one of the deeper shades of blue not only cozies up a space, it adds an air of dependability, too. Deeper blues suggest trust, so they're just right for any room where friends come to share secrets.

8
LIGHT BLUES

Calm, cool, and collected. That sums up the blues that evoke a cloudless sky or the most tranquil ocean. In a room such as a study or bedroom, where relaxation is your main mission, light blue walls go a long way toward instilling a sense of serenity and peace.

Call it a crowd-pleaser. More people—men and women—**pick blue** as their **favorite color**, making it a **perfect hue** for a room that enjoys mixed company.

9

PURPLE

Part mysterious, part majestic, purple is all bold and has a way of stirring the senses to boot. Small sitting areas and comfortable dining rooms—the more intimate, the better—are perfect spots for regal purple walls to reign.

10

LAVENDER

The softer side of purple is often partnered with pinks, yellows, and greens. But even on its own, lavender can pretty up a room. Paired with white, lavender walls convey all the elegance—without any of the pomp—that a deeper purple scheme may communicate. And you can't help but feel like a kid again when fun-loving pastels like lavender are in play.

11
BLACK

Black may be the last color to come to mind when you're thinking about wall color. But its unmatched ability to add sophistication to an environment should make you think again. Especially effective in a bathroom or bedroom, black walls don't just set the stage—they steal the show.

Ask anyone who wears a suit on a regular basis: **When you** want to convey a **touch of class,** you can't go wrong with **black.**

group
efforts

When it comes to **paintings, photographs,** and most other pieces of wall decor, one is the **loneliest number.** Of course that isn't to say that solo acts can't make **attractive additions** to your room. A single, beautifully framed mirror, for example, may be **all you need** to bring new life to the area over your mantel or **that certain spot** in your hallway. Much trickier, however, is **assembling** a collection in which elements not only work well with the others in the group, but also work **as a whole** to accent the rest of the room. Here, **trusting** your **instincts** and daring to do things a bit differently is key. When you do, you're on your way toward a **successful partnership** and a stunning display.

12

MIRROR, MIRROR …

...on the wall, what's the freshest look of all? Full-mirrored walls, which tend to be overpowering, are a thing of the past. By hanging a series of smaller mirrors instead, you'll get the same illusion of roominess, without it feeling so intrusive.

13

FACE FORWARD
In a thoroughly modern home such as this one, no one will make faces at a slightly avant-garde photo grouping. The 20 prints, hung to form a square, not only contribute to the overall boxy theme but also ensure eye contact at the end of a long hallway.

14
FLOWER PATCH

If a little romance is what you're after, say it with flowers. A quintet of botanical prints, paired with an antique photo in a carved-wood floral frame, will make a room you can't help but want to cuddle up in.

15

A TOUCH OF BRASS

They're most commonly used to hold the carpet in place on stair treads. But when mounted to the wall, brass rods such as this one can also support a dangling photo gallery in a very elegant way.

16

SOMETHING OLD, SOMETHING NEW

An old door or any other architectural find can have a second life, thanks to its ornamental value. Fragments, the decorating term for salvaged building parts, are often fabulous central pieces for groupings. Surrounding artwork should have a similar feel; notice these pictures' fine lines.

17

OUT OF AFRICA

If you pick up an interesting piece while on a trip—even if the trip is just to a store that carries imports—welcome it into your home by making it the center of an arrangement that enhances its ethnic flare. This Moroccan mirror is in good company encircled by ornaments usually hung at a home's front door as a blessing.

18

STOP AND STAIR

Mismatched mirrors make a trip up the stairs a time for reflection. Including numerous pieces in all shapes and sizes further raises the grouping's impact.

19
EMPTY INSIDE

Sometimes pretty antique frames are best left alone, drawing attention to only themselves. Hanging them in an irregular pattern makes the arrangement all the more surprising.

20
PHOTO OP

These two rows of small moldings not only mimic the larger molding overhead but also allow for many points of interest in what could have been a boring hallway. A bonus: Photos propped against the wall can be updated more easily than those nailed in place.

21
SHELF LIFE

When you own a collection this colorful, you don't want to keep it behind closed cupboard doors. Place like-colored pottery on a trio of shelves to enliven a tucked-away corner of your kitchen.

22
HAVE A SEAT

The kids may have outgrown their favorite chairs, but the chairs are just as useful as ever when hung as whimsical wall elements in a colorful room.

23
KEEN SLATES

If a big old bulletin board seems too distracting in your space, try hanging a few smaller slates in succession. Their small size makes them just right for assigning one to each family member.

24
HOOK, LINE, AND TINKER

With an ever-changing art collection, you could spend a lot of time spackling. Hanging frames from decorative hooks attached to a picture molding high on the wall makes for easier updating. Authentic Victorian picture hangers are hard to find, so try gluing antique drawer pulls onto S-hooks to get the look. Then dangle tassels for an added touch.

25
BOARD ROOM
Hanging a variety of antique board games on the walls not only showcases your collecting efforts, it also creates a unique grouping. Framed posters, newspapers, and other flat collections can also fill up a room.

26
COLLECTIVE SIGNS

In a laid-back atmosphere like this one, old-time trade signs fit right in. Hung as if puzzle pieces, the collection makes great use of the room's unusual wall space and sends a clear message of character.

27
WELL COMPOSED

Musical instruments no longer in use can enjoy a repeat performance as wall decor. Here, the artistic prints harmonize well with the woodwinds and strings, making for an arrangement that truly hits a high note.

28

ALL TOGETHER NOW

This arrangement is especially attention-getting because the mantel decor appears to be part of it. The tall topiaries play a key role, filling in space and bringing the eye upward.

29
RED PLATE SPECIAL

The hands-down easiest way to create an instantly engaging arrangement is to hang a plate rack. Pretty pieces placed on it can't help but get noticed. And outfitting it with a coordinated collection such as this one is effortless.

small
wonders

Sometimes, it is the little things that mean a lot, especially when you're talking about home decor. Colorful knobs can kick boring cabinetry up a notch. Fancy ceiling fixtures can add interest on high. And stamps and stencils can perk up once-plain walls. But ask anyone versed in even the basics of home improvement, and they'll likely give you fair warning: Just because your additions are small in stature doesn't necessarily mean that your project will be small in scale. Occasionally, however, a relatively tiny time commitment—say, a weekend or less—can result in a big boost to a living space. Whether you're looking to transform one wall or all four in a room, you'll be amazed by the difference a simple stamping or stenciling project can make.

30
AMAZING LACE

This wall owes its lacy look to a rather unusual stencil: the fabric that served as its inspiration. For this project, a 3-yard length of lace fabric was suspended from a rod hung at ceiling height and about 5 feet from the wall. A lacy shadow cast on the wall with the help of an overhead projector was used as a painting guide.

31

FERN BELIEVER

A border that borrows from nature is sure to be a perennial favorite. First, divide the wall into three sections. For an 8-foot wall, the bottom section should be at least 36 inches tall; the border, 8 inches. After painting three complementary colors, install chair rails. Then let the stamping begin, positioning the leaves close to the bottom rail and turning the stamp slightly each time. Not a fern fan? Any old stamp will do, as long as it measures at least 3 inches.

32
TWO-TIMER

Glaze gives this space its good looks. First, the entire wall was coated white. With a hard-lead pencil, a horizontal line was drawn 38 inches up from the floor. Red glaze was painted below the line. Then the flower and paisley patterns were stamped in place. Once the red glaze was dry, neutral and white glazes were mixed and blotted onto the wall with a damp mitt (*inset*).

33
SQUARE DANCE

This bubble-esque effect is perfect for a bathroom. Begin by cutting a square in the center of lightweight poster board (the inset shows a 3-inch square). Cut with a crafts knife and a metal ruler, making sure the square's edges are parallel with the poster board's. Seal the stencil with polyurethane spray so it can be wiped clean. For iridescent squares, use metallic spray paint.

34
BED HEAD

Only have a bed frame? Paint a headboard directly on the wall. Mask the design and paint it (*inset*). Then scatter stenciled daisies for a fanciful final touch.

A **row of blossoms** dances around the room to create a fanciful chair rail. With **cheerful blooms** like these encircling them, your guests are guaranteed to be in **good spirits.**

35
GONE TO POTS
The whimsical, floating flowerpots make this dining area a less serious space. For the entire scheme to match perfectly, first purchase the stencil paint and then have wall paint custom-colored to match.

36
ROLE REVERSAL
These golden scrolls were created using a single stencil twice. After paint was applied to create one side of the scroll, the stencil was flipped over to make the other side of the pattern.

1

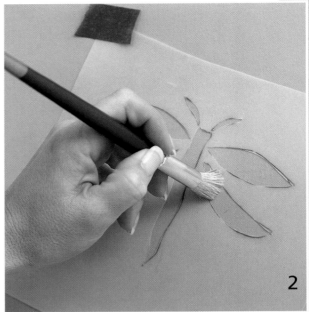

2

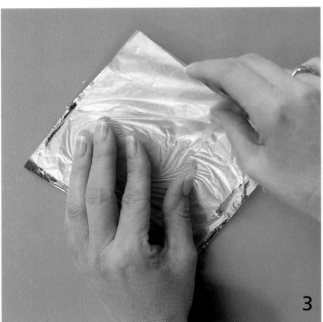

3

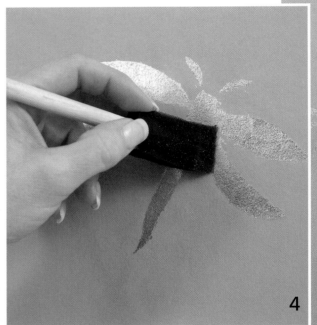

4

37

FLY ON THE WALL

Set your walls aflutter with whimsical silver dragonflies. An entire room may be overkill, so choose the most prominent wall as the place you'll set the flitters free. First, paint the wall with two coats of latex paint. Draw a simple dragonfly design on paper, then tape stencil acetate over the drawing and cut out the design with a crafts knife (*photo 1*). Lightly spray the stencil with stencil adhesive. Using the room photo at *right* as a guide, press the stencil onto the wall. Apply foiling glue for three to five designs at a time, using a stencil brush (*photo 2*). Next, apply silver leaf to the foiling glue. To prevent the silver leaf from crumbling or sticking to your fingers when you press it to the design, lay a piece of waxed paper over the foil sheet. Lift the waxed paper and the silver leaf from the packaging and gently press the silver-leaf sheet to the adhesive with your fingertips (*photo 3*). Brush off excess silver leaf with the sponge brush (*photo 4*). Repeat the process until you're satisfied with the overall dragonfly design. Finish your project by sealing the surface with polyurethane varnish. Use a short-nap roller.

The flies have it: an ability to instantly capture your attention with their silvery sheen. The effect is pure magic.

strokes
of genius

To paint or not to paint? That may be your question. An old standby, paint is the medium most often called upon to wake up walls, especially when the job needs to be accomplished in a jiffy. Once you've chosen your color (see the color chapter, Rooms with a Hue, for pointers on that), you're ready to roll. But paint doesn't always have to be just one coat. On the following pages, you'll find numerous ways paint can be used as a tool, part of a treatment, or a technique that goes beyond a single-color process. Make new walls look old, show your stripes, and learn what a difference a glaze makes. Your walls will be so original, you'll be floored.

38

DEAR OL' PLAID

A plaid paint job gives this bathroom nook pizzazz. To get the wavy effect of the plaid stripes, use a razor blade to cut the edges of painter's tape while it's still on the roll. Mask each stripe with the tape before painting for an uneven edge every time. The result is a more relaxed, casual look.

39

SQUARE CASE

Love quilts? Then paint a five-color patchwork pattern directly on the wall. Using a T-square or ruler, mark off a 24-inch square. Then divide that square into four 12-inch squares. Next make each of the smaller squares a frame by measuring 1½ inches in from each edge. Miter the corners; then draw another 1-inch frame inside. Finish the pattern by drawing four diamonds inside the frames.

40
SQUIGGLE ROOM

Get a wallpaper look—without having to paste—by painting sweet scrolls. Before putting paintbrush to wall, use chalk to lightly freehand-draw the S shapes onto the surface. Move your entire arm rather than just your hand for the smoothest strokes. Attach comma shapes and C shapes the same way to complete the effect.

space awaits anyone willing to **experiment with paint.**

41
STRIPE TWO
Create this chair-rail effect by first dividing the wall into two horizontal color bars. Then define the dividing line with hand-painted stripes in lighter, coordinating shades.

42
SPONGE JOB

When a solid color just won't do, choose a couple of hues and sponge-paint your wall instead. In this room, the technique lends an open, airy effect that's reminiscent of the desert sky. A single wash of blue paint wouldn't have produced the same outdoorsy feel.

43
PLASTER CLASS

If you feel ambitious, use plaster instead of paint. The polished Venetian plaster on these walls was chosen for its ability to reflect light and lend texture. Apply four coats of custom-tinted plaster and then burnish the surface with a trowel to bring out sheen and contrast. Let the surface cure during the workweek. When the weekend arrives, tape off stripes at approximately 10-inch intervals. Lighten the plaster mixture previously used, then apply a skim coat with a metal spackling knife to create stripes. After burnishing the stripes, let the walls dry and apply a coat of wax. Test this process and perfect your technique on a scrap of wallboard or plywood before you start work on the living room walls.

44
ROUGHIN' IT

Pressing a rough material into wet glaze textures a wall with ease. Cover your finger with a lint-free cloth to trace the shapes. Due to the glaze's quick drying time, this wall was painted in 17-inch-square sections. Then 16-inch squares of unprimed artist's canvas were pressed into the sections to create a grid. The curved lines were also drawn in while the glaze was still wet.

45

PINNED DOWN

Because the vertical lines were painted freehand with a small brush, this look isn't as stuffy as some pinstripes. For extra impact, paint the lines with metallic artist's acrylic (available in tubes at art stores)—it outshines even high-gloss wall paint.

46

BLOCK LUSTER

Not sure what technique to use on a certain space? Put a grid on it! Here, squares were taped off, then a double roller was used to blend a light base-coat color with a darker hue (*inset*). Varying the direction of the strokes produced a third marbled tone. To achieve a muted look, keep the colors just two shades apart on a paint-store color card.

47
GOOD AS BOLD

Every nook and cranny comes alive when a trio of electric hues is applied. Here, every angle was carefully considered before colors were assigned. The result is a space where cabinets, shelves, and doors all pop.

48
FOOL FOR YOU
Don't believe your eyes: These faux-paneled walls are actually made possible by an architectural illusion that started with a plain beige coat of paint. The imitation moldings were highlighted and shadowed with lighter and darker paints to give them depth.

49

AGED TO PERFECTION

Give walls a well-worn look with this technique: First, apply a coat of semigloss latex paint (here, a creamy yellow was used). Simulate the effects of aging with green artist's oil paint. Dip a brush into the paint, then into turpentine, and dab the mixture onto the wall with an artist's brush. Before it dries, wipe off the mixture, leaving a residue of color. Add more visual depth by applying umber paint and wiping it off. Apply thin coats of plaster randomly, so it appears the paint has peeled. Once dry, emphasize these areas by dipping an artist's brush first into gray artist's oil paint, next into turpentine, then outlining the plaster.

51
ABOUT A SWIRL

Surround your child's favorite characters with this wispy, whimsical background effect—or apply it to an entire wall on its own. To get the look shown here, combine 1 part blue paint, 1 part white paint, and 2 parts latex glaze for an almost translucent mixture. Working in small sections, dry-brush the glaze mixture onto white walls (avoiding any characters you may have penciled in) using circular strokes and leaving portions of the wall uncovered to simulate clouds. Before each section dries, dip a wallpaper sponge into untinted latex glaze and soften the edges, blending each section with its neighboring swirls and the wall.

52
SOMETHING FISHY

Fanciful, painted-on sea creatures make a big splash in a little bathroom. And because they're meant to look animated, even amateur artists can sketch them with success. To get this bathroom's fun, underwater effect, paint wavy, floor-to-ceiling stripes (they'll add depth to your room, too).

50
IN THE JEANS

For a casual look that works well with virtually any accessories, take a cue from your favorite duds and dress your walls with the look of denim. Here, dragging breaks up rich cobalt-blue glaze over the walls to create a subtle design of fabriclike panels. (Paint dealers sell brushes for dragging.) You can achieve other fabric effects with different base-coat and glaze colors.

53

MAKING HISTORY

This old-looking olive-branch border might evoke a Tuscan villa, but it's actually made possible by a technique called a negative finish. A top coat of glaze is applied unevenly—so the underneath color peeks out—then wiped away with a wall comb (available at crafts stores) and pencil erasers while still wet, revealing more of the color beneath.

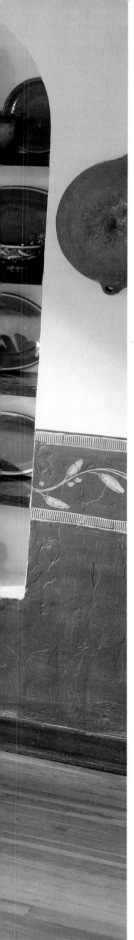

54
WELL-ROUNDED

Scalloped edges make this tall painted wainscoting a sunny addition to the room. Thanks to a tinted glaze, which is more transparent than paint, the bold color isn't at all overpowering. Begin by diluting a small amount of latex paint with water and using it to mark a level line 63 inches up from the floor, placing hash marks every 5 inches (paint should be used to mark guidelines, as pencil lines show through light colors). Trace a saucer to get a smooth curve between the hashes. Finally, fill in the curves—and the rest of the bottom half of the wall—with glaze.

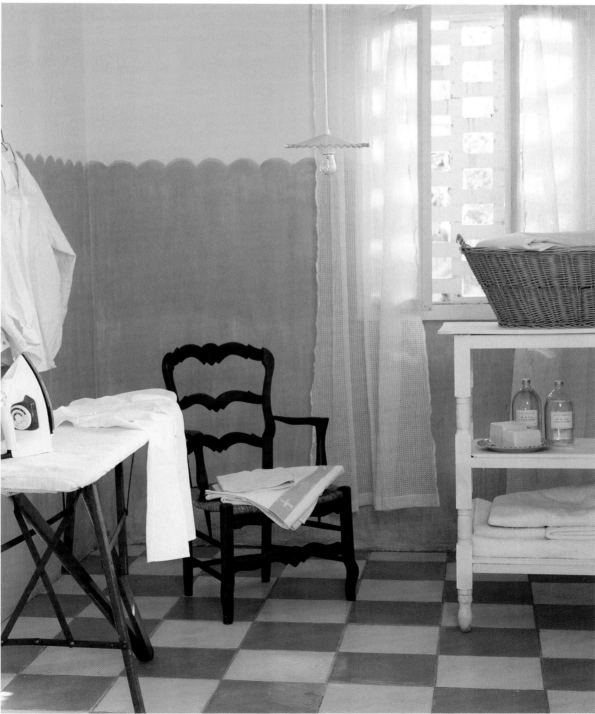

curtain call

Why should windows have **all the fun?** Whether it's used as a **temporary solution** until you can finally get to that time-consuming wallpapering project, or it's just another way for you to **work the unexpected into your home,** fabric can be a fantastic wall-covering option. When hung on a wall, **curtains, quilts, and the like** add major warmth to a space for minimum effort. So go ahead, **swatch and learn.**

55
UNDER COVER

Put cracks, chips, and other wall troubles easily out of sight behind a curtain. Simple cotton prints and coordinates work best as cover-ups. Here, colorful pegs also add whimsy.

56
GETTING WARMER

Your quilt may keep you cozy during the winter, but when it's this pleasing to the eye, why not hang it in a prominent area of your home year-round? Quick tip: Rather than centering a textile on the wall, hang it as you would a painting or a print, with the center of the work just below eye level. Hang larger quilts a little lower, so they don't come too close to the ceiling.

57

GOT GINGHAM?

No, it's not wallpaper:
These plaid panels are
upholstered. First, batting
was applied to the walls
with a combination
of spray adhesive and
staples. Then the fabric
panels were stapled in
place (matching cording
was glued along the
edges to hide the staples).
The result will make any
powder room proud.

58

SO DREAMY

A better night's sleep can't be too far away with a charming valance that suggests a canopy. And this one is so simple to put together; you can do it in an hour or so, using only a store-bought valance and curtain panels. It's quick and inexpensive, so you can rest easy.

59

PATCH AT 'EM

While this quilt would have been just as pretty as a bedcovering, its impact is intensified when it's hung on the wall behind the bed instead. In a room like this one made up of muted colors, the quilt's pink patchwork makes it a strong focal point.

You don't want a room that's cut from the **same cloth** as everyone else's. Fabric—a rather unusual yet winning wall-covering selection—will make your space a **standout** for sure.

60
NATURAL ATTRACTION

Create an area of interest in a large room by tacking and draping cotton fabric at ceiling height on one wall. You'll need the fabric to be twice the length of the wall to achieve a soft drape. Artwork can be hung right through the cloth.

hanging around

Wallpaper has gotten a bad rap. It's difficult, some people say, and messy. But hanging wallpaper well simply takes **practice and patience.** Without proper planning, you could end up with seams in **conspicuous places** or, worse, a pattern that doesn't match up. But wallpapering doesn't have to be a daunting process. If you **start small**—say, with borders alone or a room with few windows—you can **build your skills** and graduate to bigger and more complicated projects. Having a partner **helps.** With one person cutting and the other applying, you're more likely to **catch a wrinkle in time.**

61
WHAT LIES BENEATH

Yes, you can perk up your paneled room with a wallpaper cover-up. The key to the project's success is a heavy-duty liner paper (available where wallpaper is sold), which is hung horizontally before your decorative paper. If your paneling has grooves ¼ inch deep or more, fill them in with caulk first. By choosing textured wallpaper or pronounced patterns, you'll disguise grooves even more.

before

 62

THE STRAIGHT AND NARROW

Borders make sophisticated stripes when hung upright. You need a pattern that looks as nice vertically as it does horizontally; geometric patterns generally work well. We capped this treatment off at about 65 inches, plate-rail height, and topped it with a plain molding.

 63

CAMEO ROLE

Favorite images can become wall coverings if you seal them to the wall with a decoupage medium. (One warning: This treatment is more permanent than traditional wallpaper.) After deciding on pictures and placement, brush the medium over the back of each image and press it to the wall. Smooth it with your fingers, then seal with the same medium, extending it just beyond the image onto the wall. Once it dries, apply a second coat.

 64

CAUSING A SCENE

Toile is one of the busiest patterns out there, so your instinct may be to keep it out of small spaces. Don't. Its finely etched lines actually can open up a room. Paper the walls with it and add as many accents as you like. Toile looks best in abundance.

65
FINE DINING

Supper can be super when you're seated in a room that's this pleasing to the eye. Here, three papers commingle, but one is given the most prominence. By running one paper two-thirds to three-fourths of the way up the wall, the effect for seated guests is cozy, not cluttered. The dominant pattern is divided from the other two papers by a molding. The wide border then serves as a backdrop for photos that rest atop the molding.

66
THREE'S COMPANY

Mixing three wallpaper patterns effectively isn't easy, but it can be done. First, select one dominant pattern (here, it's the border), and make sure part of its color scheme is reflected in the other two prints. Keep the darkest background on bottom; balance with a lighter-colored paper on top.

A CUT ABOVE

What could have been your trash is really your treasure. Before tossing leftover wallpaper, consider the pattern. If the design is such that elements can be cut out (as is the case with these diamond-shaped botanical prints), you can give paper new life as a decorative border. Creating cutouts makes coordinating a bathroom and an adjacent bedroom easy.

68

LONG DIVISION

Create panels by hanging your borders two ways. Divide the wall into 22- to 26-inch-wide segments. Apply the vertical borders; then add a horizontal one at chair-rail height.

69

UPWARD BOUND

Showcase a shelf or two with a coordinating wallpaper. This striped paper, which draws the eye upward, makes the arrangements all the more engaging.

Torn brown kraft paper, disguised by interior latex paint, has an **amazing effect** on walls. The best part: Wrinkles only add to the **treatment's charm.**

70
ALL TORN UP

When is wallpaper not really wallpaper? When it's brown kraft paper (available at art supply and crafts stores) transformed into a winning and less costly wall covering. Start by rolling out sheets of the kraft paper on a large work surface. Drop blobs of interior latex paints that will combine for your desired color. (Here, two tones of orange and white paint were blended.) Using a large brush, paint the paper. After it dries, brush on a wash of gold metallic tints mixed into a clear glaze base. Once completely dry, tear the paper into good-size pieces and apply to the wall with regular wallpaper paste. Position straight-edge pieces along the ceiling and baseboards and use the remaining pieces to fill, overlapping or butting edges as you go. With a wallpaper brush or soft cloth, smooth the kraft paper in place. To protect the treatment and make it durable, seal the walls with a water-base varnish.

71

FEELING GROOVY

Embossed paper hides flaws in your walls especially well. To enhance its texture, try painting it, then removing some of the wet paint with a squeegee to reveal the high spots.

72
CONTINENTAL DRIFT

You could scour the globe for a more creative wall covering, but you may not find one. Large maps can work just like real wallpaper—just apply paste to the back of the map and the wall. Given that maps only come in one sheet, you may have to take some geographical liberties.

73
JUST BEACHY

When you don't need to commission an artist, a mural can be a day at the beach. Here, wallpaper was hung before the border, which was aligned with the mattress top to keep it in clear view. Narrow molding was added to further highlight the beachy-keen scene.

into the woods

Unless your home is custom-built, chances are it's a bit more plain than you'd like, as today's builders tend to favor the flat over the architecturally interesting. But just because your walls weren't blessed with bounteous beauty from the beginning doesn't mean they have to stay the way they are. If you have a hammer and a few other simple tools, such as a saw and perhaps a drill, you can stage a molding makeover that not only enhances your walls but also dresses up your entire room. And you don't need to be a master woodworker to do it. With the help of precut moldings (home improvement centers offer a wide array)—and a little inspiration—your room will be on its way to another dimension.

74
PICTURE-PERFECT

Usually hung at the ceiling, crown molding and a wallpaper border, *above* and *left*, are brought down to just above the tabletop, creating an attractive ledge to display photographs. Because of its muted tones, this border complements the picture rail.

75

SHELF LIFE

Bookcase, begone. Reading materials, cherished collectibles, and even framed photographs reach new heights with the construction of a display shelf like this one. Fabricated from 1×6 boards, wainscoting 5½ feet high is topped by a 5½-inch-deep shelf. Pegs give clothing a reason to hang around.

76
CUT IT OUT

Don't fret; you can do a fretwork project like this original wainscoting yourself. All you need is a jigsaw. (Warning: This project will take more than one weekend if you decide to get intricate with your design or have a lot of wall to cover.) Here, a pair of geometric motifs was set into grids of 1×2s and 1×3s. The fretwork was cut in ⅜-inch particleboard (other sheet material would work), and the framing is ¾-inch material.

77
LATTICE ALONE

The eye-catching woodwork in this living room borrows from the garden out back. Floor-to-ceiling lattice, which can be purchased in sheets and cut to fit virtually any space in your home, frames an entryway and makes the neutral-colored room more interesting.

78
MEASURING UP

Unique wainscoting like this, made up of a collection of different-colored vintage yardsticks (or some just stained to look that way), signals that character is afoot in your home. As a rule, small spaces are best for this project, due to the number of yardsticks needed.

79

HANG RAIL

Chair rails aren't just for rooms with traditional seating. Hung in a bathroom and peppered with pegs, they also can function as contemporary towel racks.

80
THE GREAT DIVIDE

If your tall walls could use a break, vertical and horizontal moldings used together can help. Once you've determined the height where you'll hang your horizontal molding (the one shown is 20 inches from the ceiling), be sure to treat the wall above and below the line differently.

added touches

Finally your paint job has dried evenly. Your wallpaper paste has adhered properly. Your molding makeover bears witness that you paid attention in wood shop. But now that all is said and hung, maybe your wall still could use a little something extra. Or maybe you're searching for a solution for a hard-to-dress spot. Whether you need a place to post your notes, hang your hat, or display your most treasured possessions, you'll find a project suited to your needs on the following pages. Some can be accomplished in a few hours; others—be warned—may take more than one weekend with drying time included. But each will make your room all the more charmed, we're sure.

81

A ROLL IN THE CLAY

If you can't find the exact tiles you have in mind, why not make them yourself? In two weekends (drying time prohibits this project from being finished in one), you can create a look that's all your own. Pair your tiles with store-bought ones in a mosaic backsplash and turn up the character in your kitchen.

1

2

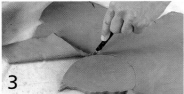

3

4

5

6

WHAT YOU NEED

- Earthenware or terra-cotta clay (available at crafts stores)
- Underglaze in desired color (available at ceramics supply shops)
- Overglaze in desired colors
- Mastic
- Premixed grout
- Polyurethane or other sealer
- Rolling pin
- Crafts knife
- Tracing paper
- Marking pen
- Unbleached canvas
- Paintbrushes
- Putty knife
- Hammer and towel
- Cloth or sponge
- Latex gloves

STEP-BY-STEP

1. Roll a chunk of clay out like dough on the unbleached canvas to ¼ inch thick (*photo 1*).

2. Draw your design (shown at *left* is a salad bowl, 6 inches wide) on tracing paper with a marking pen. Place template over clay. Cut through the paper and into the clay with a crafts knife to lightly incise details and outline (*photo 2*).

3. Remove template and finish cutting the tile outline (*photo 3*). Let clay dry fully (it will take two or three days). Take it to a ceramics shop to fire per their instructions (the store may charge a small fee, often 50 cents to $1 per tile.) Paint tile with underglaze; fire again. Paint tile with overglaze (*photo 4*); fire again. Apply two or three coats of sealer to protect the finish; let dry between coats.

4. When you've made all the needed custom tiles, you're ready to adhere them to the wall. Black ready-made tiles fill in between the handmade pieces shown, but any color will do. Stick to one color that showcases your homemade tiles and doesn't fight them for attention. Cover the commercial tiles with a towel, then break them with a hammer into small, irregularly shaped pieces. Determine the placement of each custom tile on the wall.

5. Apply mastic to the back of each handmade tile with a putty knife; press into place. Hold for a few seconds, wiggling tile a little to secure it to the wall. Using the same method, apply the broken black pieces to fill in the spaces (*photo 5*). Let dry 24–48 hours.

6. Following manufacturer's directions, apply grout to the wall with a gloved hand (*photo 6*). Push it into the crevices between tiles. Wait 15–30 minutes for grout to set. With a damp cloth or sponge, wipe off the surface of the tiles to remove any grout residue before it dries. Allow grout to cure for the period recommended by the manufacturer, then brush on two or three coats of sealer.

82

GONE TO PIECES

The whole family could chip in on this backsplash. Begin by gathering plates and tiles that fit your desired color scheme. Tiles can be purchased new; to cut costs, try estate and garage sales for old dishes (it doesn't matter if they're cracked or broken a bit). Once you've amassed a selection to your liking, break the tiles and plates simply by dropping them on the ground (you may want to make this an outdoor activity). For best results, pencil a design on the wall, noting the appropriate placement for each color before you apply the tiles with thin-set adhesive. Chances are your backsplash will be a smashing success.

STEP-BY-STEP

1. Place a straightedge diagonally across one metal square, lining up at opposite corners; bend the free corner up slightly to crease the square.

2. Using a drill and a ⅛-inch twist bit, drill one hole in the corner opposite the bent-up half and one hole in each adjacent corner of the flat half, as shown. Repeat for the remaining 19 squares.

3. Measure and mark a 2-inch-wide frame around the perimeter of the plywood. Position the metal squares inside the framed area with the holes in the bottom and left corners. Working from the bottom row up and carefully aligning each square, attach them to the plywood with wood screws.

4. Paint the plywood frame as desired. Secure screw eyes into the top of the plywood 6 inches from each edge; thread ribbon through the screw eyes to create a hanger.

83
NOTE WORTHY

No thumbtacks are needed for this message board. Instead, squares of thin aluminum sheet metal are mounted in a neat grid to snag important paperwork. The plywood frame can be decorated any which way you like.

84

SO FLY

Put away the swatter. This dragonfly, a piece of art in its own right, is also a fun way to show off photos. The insect's body is fashioned from lengths of aluminum wire; the binder clip attached to its tail holds pictures in place.

WHAT YOU NEED
- 72-inch piece of aluminum electric-fence wire
- 40-inch length of 24-gauge aluminum wire
- Wire cutters
- Two pencils
- One small binder clip
- Spray paint that adheres to metal

STEP-BY-STEP

1. Cut a 36-inch-long piece of fence wire. Lay one pencil perpendicularly across the middle of the wire. Gently bend each end of the wire around the pencil and twist together tightly twice to form a loop for the dragonfly's head; remove the pencil. Place two pencils side by side after the twists. Wrap the wire ends around the pencils and twist tightly twice to form a slightly larger loop for the body; remove the pencils. Using one pencil, repeat the wrap-and-twist technique to form two additional loops for the body.

2. Twist the remaining wire together to form the tail, stopping 1 inch from the ends. Twist the wire ends around one metal handle of the binder clip. Curl the tail so the clip opening faces up.

3. Cut two 8-inch-long pieces and two 10-inch-long pieces of fence wire. Bend each in the middle to form a U shape, creating four wings. Position one wing of each size, the larger on top, on each side of the body. Wrap the loose ends around the body once to secure in place.

4. Cut four 10-inch-long pieces of 24-gauge wire. Wrap the end of one piece once around the body where the first wing is attached. Wind the wire back and forth around the outside of the wing in a zigzag pattern. Wrap the end once around the wing wire; snip off any excess. Repeat with the remaining wings.

5. Spray-paint the completed dragonfly any color you like; let dry.

6. Hang over a tack in the wall.

85

POST OFFICE

Prevent papers from piling up in your office—or anywhere—by installing a corkboard border. By hanging it at chair-rail height and banding it top and bottom with a wallpaper trim, you'll create a point of interest in your space, too. First, attach cork squares (available at home centers) directly to the wall with a thin bead of construction adhesive. The top of the cork should be about 4 feet from the floor, just above seated eye level. A wallpaper border no more than half the width of squares will result in the most pleasing proportion; look for one that also reflects the feel of your room (here we chose one with computer terms). Using wallpaper paste, mount the wallpaper border along the top and bottom of the cork squares.

86
BEHIND CLOSED DOORS

It can serve as a homework hot spot or a preferred place to doodle. Whatever its function, a dry-erase board will likely draw any kid who wants to make a mark. Bringing it into a room where the family gathers makes it more useful but doesn't do much for the decor. This one was designed to make mother and child happy: It's recessed a few inches, so doors that match the room's other cabinetry can conceal works in progress when company comes.

87
WORD PLAY

What a way to gather the gang! A creative collection such as this one definitely puts the focus on the family. Instead of staging the same-old photo gallery, mix it up with mismatched frames—some hung, some situated on shelves—and family-friendly quotes painted directly on the wall.

88

WRITE ON

Chalk it up to a clever idea: With blackboard paint (applied like conventional wall paint), you can construct a board big enough to broadcast all your family's commitments. It even comes in an array of colors, so your board doesn't need to be black at all. Either roll the paint directly on the wall or apply it to fiberboard that has been cut to desired size. One coat covers most surfaces; expect a drying time of about four hours. If you do use fiberboard, frame it with picture molding. Paint or stain the molding pieces and miter the corners. Attach the fiberboard to the frame with brads or small nails. Secure the frame to the wall with screws, making sure to hit wall studs for security.

STEP-BY-STEP

1. Measure halfway down the side of one sap bucket; draw a 1×8-inch rectangular slot parallel to the bottom of the bucket. Drill a starting hole in the rectangle with a drill and a twist bit, and cut out the opening with a saber saw. Repeat with the other bucket, measuring carefully to position the slot in the same place.

2. Paint the 1×6 or 1×8 board (depending on the bucket size) as desired; let dry. Slide the board into the slots in the sap buckets one at a time.

3. To mount, hold the assembled shelf against the wall and mark inside the lip of each bucket where it touches the wall. Remove the board from the buckets, and drill a hole at each mark. Reassemble the shelf and hang with nails into the wall studs.

89
WALL FLOWERS

Don't just put your flowers on the shelf—make them part of it. In addition to holding darling buds, these sap buckets double as brackets for the simple shelf between them. You can use old buckets or buy new ones at a crafts store and paint them to look worn. Either way, make sure they're watertight before you hang them.

90
IRONY

At first glance, this Victorian wrought-iron towel rack looks like an antiques-store treasure. Instead, it's faux ironwork, painted on the wall above some black utility hooks. For a different look, paint an Art Deco design in silver to represent brushed aluminum or stainless steel, then install plain metal hooks. Brass-color paint and brass hooks would work, too.

WHAT YOU NEED

- Ruler
- Drill
- French curve
- Assorted round and flat paintbrushes
- Black and white acrylic paints (tube or liquid)
- Metal utility hooks

STEP-BY-STEP

1. Mark positions for three black metal utility hooks on the wall. Drill pilot holes for the screws.

2. Temporarily attach the hooks to the wall, and sketch the outline of the wrought-iron design on the wall with a pencil. Remove the hooks.

3. Draw the wrought-iron design into the outline. Use the ruler and French curve to keep the lines relatively smooth.

4. Use a round brush to paint the wrought-iron design with black acrylic paint. Keep the edges straight for a realistic look. Let the black paint dry.

5. Mix black and white paints to make a light gray. Using a flat shader brush, highlight the faux wrought iron with the gray paint to add dimension. Apply the highlights with an almost-dry brush, building them up as necessary to avoid a harsh look. Add a few white highlights to enhance the effect.

6. After the paint dries, attach the hooks to the wall.

91
FLOWER POP

Empower your flowers by giving them a platform all their own. A small ledge boxed in with matching materials creates a stage of sorts that makes your fresh flowers look even fresher or gives artificial blooms new life. To make the shelf, cut two birch boards long enough to hold your display. The shelf shown uses a ½-inch-thick piece for the top and a ¾-inch-thick piece for the back. Join them with a butt joint, and attach the shelf to the wall with nails or picture hooks. Make the frame from the same birch boards, using miter cuts at the joints. Not inclined to make it yourself? Purchase a shelf and frame that complement each other. Whichever way you create your showcase, paint the wall inside the frame to give the arrangement prominence.

92
FRAME BY FRAME

Want to put something clever on your wall but coming up empty? Take a cue from your cluelessness and simply hang a row of identical frames. The look is especially effective when painted-on color is all they call attention to; just go for the most obvious hues in your room's palette, or the frames will stick out rather than accent your decor. Or to create additional interest, hang a group of mismatched frames painted the same color. Use a ruler and a level to make sure your frames are positioned evenly. Prevent the frames from shifting by nailing the frames directly to the wall.

93
PERSONAL SPACE

Old photographs, family heirlooms, and other treasured keepsakes can be neatly housed in a newfangled shadow box—no glass needed. First, hold a standard frame against the wall and mark around the inside directly on the wall with a hard-lead pencil. Then paint slightly beyond the lines so the frame opening will cover the painted area. Nail your frame in place, making sure to cover up (and paint over) your nail holes. As a rule, it's best to use small nails for objects hung inside; use mounting tape for positioning photos within the frame.

94
INITIAL RESPONSE

For a truly personal touch, frame a monogrammed handkerchief or napkin, which can be folded to fit neatly into a frame. Pairing an old, worn frame with a delicate linen makes for a most charming combination.

95
HANG ON

Bring garden style to your bathroom, kitchen, or hallway with a lovely lattice shelf. Making it requires only basic woodworking skills: Start by building a 13×38-inch frame using 1×3 boards. Using a handsaw, cut a piece of purchased 1-inch lattice 37 inches long; then secure to the back of the frame using brads or a staple gun. Secure architectural brackets to the frame by screwing through the back of the frame and into the brackets. Cut a 39-inch-wide shelf from a 1×8 board, rounding the corners with a jigsaw if desired. Screw through the top of the shelf into the frame and brackets. Paint white, and add hooks (the more antique-looking, the better) to the center of the panel.

96
CHECK IT OUT

A lattice mirror is a good-looking addition to any entryway. To make it, start with a lattice panel in your desired size and then frame the entire panel in decorative molding. Miter the molding at the corners. Add a 1×3 frame around the molding using glue and finishing nails. For an even easier project, insert lattice into a purchased picture frame with the glass removed. To finish either project, paint the frame and lattice white, and let dry. Then secure a mirror to the center of the lattice panel with plastic clips.

WHAT YOU NEED

- 23-inch length of 1×6 pine
- 23-inch strip of 1×2 pine
- Dinner plate and pencil
- Scroll saw and drill
- Medium- and fine-grit sandpaper and tack cloth
- Hammer and nails
- Acrylic paints in cream and dusty pink
- Foam brush
- Three vintage forks
- Drill
- Screwdriver and six screws
- Needle-nose pliers
- Two sawtooth hangers

STEP-BY-STEP

1. Beginning at the center of the 1×6, use a dinner plate and pencil to draw scallops along one long edge. Cut along the scalloped lines with a scroll saw.

2. Drill four 1-inch holes through the rack, referring to the photo for placement. Sand the scalloped piece and the pine strip with medium-grit, then fine-grit sandpaper. Remove the sanding dust with a tack cloth. Nail the strip to the long, straight edge of the scalloped piece t o make a ledge.

3. Base-coat all surfaces of the rack with cream paint and let it dry. Then paint the rack dusty pink and let it dry. For a distressed look, lightly sand the rack to expose the base coat and some areas of raw wood. Remove the sanding dust with a tack cloth.

4. Arrange the forks on the rack, spacing them evenly. Mark the screw locations with pencil marks on each side of the fork tines 1 inch below the ledge. Drill starter holes for the screws; then partially drive the screws into the rack. Use needle-nose pliers to bend the outside fork tines around the screws. Bend the fork handles upward and then curve them out.

5. Tighten screws to secure the forks. Attach sawtooth hangers to the back of the rack.

97
FORK LIFT

This shelf is so easy to construct that you won't get bent out of shape in the process. If your kitchen doesn't have silverware to spare, fanciful forks can be found at flea markets or garage sales. Pink and cream paints make a pretty palette, but other light colors will work just as well.

98
TILE STYLE

The best part about this over-the-bed arrangement is that it can be changed at any time. Thanks to pressure-sensitive tape (you can also use hook-and-loop fastening tape), the tiles are never permanent.

99
CLOTHES MINDED

It may not be spacious, but this little ledge, reminiscent of a picket fence, can display more than you might think. Its 2-inch-deep shelf is just the spot for a special piece or two. And flowers, candles, and other accents can be clipped along its clothespin perimeter.

WHAT YOU NEED
- 27½-inch length of 2×2 lumber
- 32½×2¼-inch piece of ¼-inch plywood
- About 50 spring-clamp clothespins
- Picture-hanging hooks
- Handsaw; miter box
- Wood glue; hammer; finishing nails
- Latex paint; paintbrush

STEP-BY-STEP
1. Mount picture-hanging hooks on one side of the 2×2 lumber to form the back of the shelf.
2. Cut the plywood strip into one 28-inch-long piece (for shelf front) and two 2¼-inch-long pieces (for shelf sides). Miter each end of the front piece and one end of each side piece at a 45-degree angle. Position the pieces against the front sides of the 2×2 piece, matching the mitered corners and lining up all the bottom edges. Secure the joints with wood glue and finishing nails.
3. Position clothespin halves vertically along the plywood sides and front of the shelf. Every three to five halves, attach a whole clothespin, alternating them so some open up and some open down. Glue the flat side of each clothespin to the plywood and let dry.
4. Paint the shelf as desired. For a rustic look, wipe the loaded paintbrush on newspaper until the brush is almost dry; then apply a thin coat to the shelf, as was done on the one shown. You could also paint it with a base coat and top coat and then follow the instructions for distressing in the Fork Lift project on page 285.

100
SITTING PRETTY

Save space and cozy up your kitchen by employing this ingenious idea. A rustic farm table with benches instantly becomes a comfy banquette with the addition of cushions hung on the wall. Foam squares covered in the same fabric as the cushions hang from tabs on a slender brass curtain rod. Now you can sit back and enjoy your meal.

Better Homes and Gardens®
Creative Collection™

Director, Editorial Administration
Michael L. Maine

Editor-in-Chief
Beverly Rivers

Executive Editor Karman Wittry Hotchkiss

Editorial Manager **Art Director**
Ann Blevins Don Nickell

Copy Chief Mary Heaton
Administrative Assistant Lori Eggers
Contributing Graphic Designer Lauren Luftman
Contributing Copy Editor Wendy Wetherbee
Contributing Proofreader Joleen Ross

Vice President, Publishing Director
William R. Reed

Group Publisher Steve Levinson
Senior Marketing Manager Suzy Johnson

Meredith CORPORATION

Chairman and CEO
William T. Kerr

In Memoriam
E. T. Meredith III (1933–2003)

Publishing Group President
Stephen M. Lacy
Magazine Group President
Jack Griffin

©Meredith Corporation, 2004.
All rights reserved. Printed in the U.S.A.